SACRED
PARIS

ALSO BY SUSAN CAHILL

The Streets of Paris

Hidden Gardens of Paris

The Smiles of Rome

Desiring Italy

For the Love of Ireland

A Literary Guide to Ireland
(with Thomas Cahill)

Wise Women

WOMEN AND FICTION SERIES

Earth Angels

SACRED PARIS

A Guide to the Churches, Synagogues, and the Grand Mosque in the City of Light

SUSAN CAHILL

PHOTOGRAPHS BY MARION RANOUX

ST. MARTIN'S
GRIFFIN
NEW YORK

First published in the United States by St. Martin's Griffin,
an imprint of St. Martin's Publishing Group

SACRED PARIS. Copyright © 2022 by Susan Cahill. Photographs copyright
© 2022 by Marion Ranoux. All rights reserved. Printed in China.
For information, address St. Martin's Publishing Group,
120 Broadway, New York, NY 10271.

www.stmartins.com

Library of Congress Cataloging-in-Publication Data

Names: Cahill, Susan, author. | Ranoux, Marion, photographer.
Title: Sacred Paris : a guide to the churches, synagogues, and the grand
  mosque in the City of Light / Susan Cahill ; photographs by Marion
  Ranoux.
Other titles: Guide to the churches, synagogues, and the grand mosque in
  the City of Light
Description: First edition. | New York : St. Martin's Griffin, 2022. |
  Includes bibliographical references and index.
Identifiers: LCCN 2021047573 | ISBN 9781250239686 (trade paperback) |
  ISBN 9781250239693 (ebook)
Subjects: LCSH: Church buildings—France—Paris—Guidebooks. |
  Paris (France)—Buildings, structures, etc.—Guidebooks. |
  Synagogues,—France—Paris—Guidebooks. | Religious architecture—
  France—Paris—Guidebooks. | Paris (France)—Description and travel.
Classification: LCC DC773 .C45 2022 | DDC 944.361—dc23
LC record available at https://lccn.loc.gov/2021047573Sa

Our books may be purchased in bulk for promotional, educational, or business
use. Please contact your local bookseller or the Macmillan Corporate and
Premium Sales Department at 1-800-221-7945, extension 5442, or by email
at MacmillanSpecialMarkets@macmillan.com.

First Edition: 2022

10 9 8 7 6 5 4 3 2 1

For CONOR
BELOVED GRANDSON
And for PAMELA TAYLOR MORTON,
Dear Friend of Paris, who, knowing the beauty
and courtesy and élan of the City of Light,
has deepened the pleasure of writing this book.
In gratitude

DISCLAIMER

The Covid pandemic may have caused changes in the schedules of Masses and Sacred Music concerts in the religious institutions of Paris. The information on their websites may be out of date in mid-2022 (the publication date of *Sacred Paris*). Check websites for updates before visiting. Or visit the church, mosque, or synagogue in person to find out the new schedules of services and the Sacred Music concerts. I have walked to all the destinations featured in *Sacred Paris* and suggested the métros and routes I used in the course of many explorations over many years. The métros are still on their tracks; in the streets you find as always diversity, beauty, and mystery.

CONTENTS

x   *Contents*

SACRED
PARIS

INTRODUCTION

God is in everything, Vincent van Gogh (1853–1890) shouted up and down the hills of Montmartre. He wasn't just a solo manic-pantheist *en plein air*. Some of his fellow artists and those who came earlier and later felt the same way: Hector Berlioz, Zadoc Kahn, Henri Bergson, Olivier Messiaen, Antoine de Saint-Exupéry, Robert Bresson, to name only a few. Mystics, rabbis, philosophers, musicians, painters, filmmakers. Anonymous millions.

The great French painter Eugène Delacroix (1798–1863), whose work van Gogh adored—especially his colors—wrote in his *Journal*: "God is within us. He is the inner presence that causes us to admire the beautiful." When he listened to his friend Chopin play the piano, he said he heard God's presence descending through his fingers. For Delacroix, beauty connected us to the divine.

That intuition of a hidden living presence in the most beautiful city in the world is the focus of this book: ***Sacred Paris: A Guide to the Churches, Synagogues, and the Grand Mosque in the City of Light***. People give that hidden presence different names: God, the Sacred, the transcendent, the divine. Or it goes unnamed. For some it's conscience. Consciousness. Love.

Sacred Paris guides travelers, whether on foot or reading at home, to look for the traces of mystery in the traditional settings for prayer and worship: the churches, synagogues, and the Grand Mosque, which are also the settings for enchanting concerts of **sacred music**. This is a world often overlooked by Parisians themselves and by travelers.

There are also the untraditional—or noninstitutional—settings of the sacred, for example, the *river Seine* as seen from *Place Aragon* in early morning light. As the Seine and the centuries flowed on, both were seen almost universally from a sacred perspective. So, too, the Montmartre hills where prehistoric Celtic druids built their altars. Or the cafés all over Paris where terraces come alive in the smiles of friends as well as in the joy of lovers, strolling the quays under the night sky.

When the Enlightenment and the Revolution drew a line between what they called the sacred world—if they acknowledged its existence—and the secular world, many people, especially artists, did not connect with that bifurcated design: that was not how they saw reality. To visionaries who desired the whole picture—or just the flow of its parts in various directions—there was no line, no wall separating the universe according to abstract definitions or preconceptions. Reality was not a matter of boxy historical eras and rectangles and squares with fixed boundaries between them. Reality was unboundaried. Fluid. Incomplete. The modernist James Joyce evoked the once dominant father god as "a shout in the street."

Jocoserious Joyce was not blaspheming. On Sunday mornings he walked the Seine bridges with his friend Samuel Beckett, now and then stopping in churches, checking out masses or baptisms, still familiar from his long-ago Catholic childhood. Loving the streets and quays of Paris as he had loved the Liffey and the bridges of Dublin, he would have agreed with van Gogh—*"God is in everything"*—or, as he put it in *Finnegans Wake*, "Here Comes Everybody."

Paris is a city on a river, the sacred river Seine, whose source according to some historians and mythmakers is of divine origin, the offspring of the healing goddess Sequana. The abiding, always moving arc of the river makes all the difference to how Parisians see things. "Is it possible that all of life is like a river?" writes the poet Henri Cole. "We must either yield to it or struggle against the current."

American philosopher William James, a regular visitor to Paris from early childhood and author of *The Varieties of Religious Experience*, also noted the fluidity of things, of time itself: "This shifting of the emotional center towards loving and harmonious affections, towards 'yes, yes' and away from 'no,'" said James, is, "the love of life . . . that is the religious impulse."

When van Gogh was asked what his "theology" was, he said, "Love many things."

The word "sacred" has taken on new meanings in the decades before and after World War II. "What is still sacred after the death of God?" asks Richard Kearney, editor of *Reimagining the Sacred*. What can we call holy after Auschwitz, after the disappearance of the God of triumph and certainty?

The German martyr Dietrich Bonhoeffer, awaiting his execution in a Nazi prison, called for a future of holiness—religion—as simply a new life in existence for others. He interpreted transcendence, the sacred, as the neighbor who is within reach in any given situation.

The Polish poet Czeław Miłosz saw religion, like poetry, as "a contradiction to nihilism."

The French philosopher, political activist, and *résistante* Simone Weil, walking her native city where she was raised in a secular Jewish family (though she liked visiting churches), wrote that if Christianity is not incarnate—made flesh in the service of human beings—it is not Christianity: rigid rules have nothing to do with the sacred.

Visiting the city's various sites of worship or meditation, you will be walking (map in hand) the main geographic *quartiers* of Paris: **Île de la Cité**; **Île Saint-Louis**; **the Left Bank** and its *quartiers* (Latin Quarter, Saint-Germain); **Southern Paris** (Montparnasse); **Western Paris**; the **Right Bank** and its *quartiers* (Montmartre; the Marais); **Northern Paris**; **Northeastern Paris**; and the **Bastille**.

You will find each of these districts or *quartiers* in the **Contents**. Travelers and readers found this organization easy to follow in my books *Hidden Gardens of Paris: A Guide to the Parks, Squares, and Woodlands of the City of Light* as well as in *The Streets of Paris: Following in the Footsteps of Famous Parisians Throughout History*. As you walk, you'll find the *"Nearbys"* listed at the end of each selection: the good bistros, *librairies, pâtisseries, cinémathèques*, museums, markets, parks, wine bars, and squares, many of these out-of-the-way or off the beaten track in scruffy, bleak, ordinary *quartiers*. You'll have in mind as you walk (or take the métro or a taxi) this book's focus, the churches and synagogues in Paris, which are sometimes empty or sometimes alive with liturgy and music. You walk into a church and find an organist practicing a Bach Prelude or rockers warming up for that night's concert in *Saint-Eustache*.

It has been my pleasure to discover many of these sacred treasures and surprises on foot, in every season. Some of these settings and their works would qualify as sacred to moderns like Bonhoeffer; to the volunteers at **Médecins Sans Frontières**

(MSF) near Bastille, and at **Oxfam** in the eleventh *arrondissement*; at Secours Populaire Français (SPF, **French Popular Relief**) in the third *arrondissement*; the outreach groups who serve the needs of immigrants at **Saint-Merri** and **Saint-Ambroise**; the volunteers at the **Emmaus House** Thrift Shops; the soup kitchens that are everywhere (see the booklet *Notre bilan d'activité* at www.secourspopulaire.fr/bilan-activite).

There is not much practical help in this guidebook—the locations of salons or dry cleaners or a dentist. Hospital locations are well marked. Street markets abound, along with Monoprix and wine shops and hotels.

As you walk, you'll pass Parisians and travelers reading a book or newspaper or cell phone, people watching, sleeping, taking time out to visit with a friend in the Luxembourg. *Sacred Paris* recommends many good books related to a particular place in the city at the end of each selection. Armchair travelers can check out the titles in the Related Readings; actual travelers can read about a place or *quartier* in advance of visiting the city. I bought many of these books in the wonderful Paris *librairies*, often on the recommendation of well-read booksellers, especially in Galignani.

As much fun as it is to wander through Paris—the aimless strolling of the *flanerie* just to discover and enjoy the feast—it's essential to have a street map or two at hand, such as the Little Red Book *Paris par Arrondissements*, available at most news kiosks or bookshops; and, finally, the very usable folding map **Streetwise Paris**. You will remember the places you saw and loved (or didn't) much more vividly if you let the pages of *Sacred Paris* guide your choices and itineraries rather than shuffling and getting stuck inside a crowd, tailing a guide waving a red flag and shouting the name of the place you're passing.

Most of the churches listed in the Contents are Catholic churches because Paris has been Catholic since Clovis converted to Christianity in 496, later baptized in 508. Since then, people have known almost two millennia of Catholicism. In the sixteenth century, after endless bloody civil wars of religion between Catholics and the new Protestants (Huguenots), Paris became a mixed culture of Protestant Christian and Catholic Christian, thanks to the good sensualist and pluralist King Henri IV—who detested partisan religion.

But religious peace was always—and still is—fragile. *Sacred Paris,* however, does not focus on the city as a battleground of religious slaughter or on intellectuals' arguments about the difference between "secular" and "sacred"— though it doesn't ignore these conflicts, especially as they tore apart Paris at the time of the Revolution.

Jews have lived in Paris since the Romans and have been persecuted since the Middle Ages, which the selection about *Sainte-Chapelle* makes clear. Buddhists, Hindus, Muslims, atheists, and humanists have mingled with other religious communities, generating a mosaic of spiritual cultures over the years. Ministers, priests, rabbis, and imans now go back and forth between one another's congregations, their choirs singing out joy on religious feasts and at weekend concerts in all seasons. Some churches are empty during the week; others are SRO on special occasions: the anniversaries of the end of wars; of the Normandy invasion; of the liberation of Paris; and the birthdays of artists and heroes. Always the music of remembrance is profound and moving. Brahms's German Requiem. Verdi's choruses. Evensong at Saint-Germain-des Prés: *Écoute, Écoute! Le Seigneur marche près de toi!* Poulenc's Glorias. Concert schedules are usually posted outside and inside churches, on streetlamps, or on the websites of churches, synagogues, or mosques. (But websites are often out of date or incorrect.)

Sacred Paris includes about thirty religious places: churches, mosques, synagogues, chapels. Many are not included for the sake of brevity or because they attract tourist crowds (Sacré-Coeur). Some of the excluded ones are beautiful; some have provocative events and stories connected with them. Saint-Laurent has a lovely children's choir. Notre-Dame-de-la-Croix in Ménilmontant has beautiful wooden sculptures and the longest aisle in Paris after the Cathedral of Notre-Dame. For many years the very hidden Sainte-Marguerite claimed to possess the body of the child Louis XVII, whose heart is now in the crypt of the Basilica of Saint-Denis. The church of Saint Eugène–Sainte-Cécile is unique, a gem. Sainte-Marie des Batignolles has a striking crucifix that the poet Verlaine loved. And a visit to the sweet village of Batignolles (see *Hidden Gardens of Paris*) is well worth the métro ride. Saint-Roch is the church for sacred music and the theater; it has a good bookshop connected to it. And on and on and on. There are several hundred more gems.

Paris these days is a city in the key of diversity—atonal, rich, and original in its appetites—and more and more in its polyphonic pluralistic vision of history. Traditional religions are not as cherished as they once were, some having grown rotten with scandals or cover-ups.

Islam still remains an outsider faith in some areas, awaiting its place in more hospitable sanctuaries. The poetry of Rūmī, however, Islam's thirteenth-century poet laureate, is now heard in many sacred songs. Allah, like Yahweh and Christ, is invoked and praised. Muslims make up 10 percent of the French population. Their places of worship are more hidden away than the churches and synagogues.

To quote the wonderful British writer Richard Cobb, "Paris is the abode of love, as well as of violence. . . . Love is there all the time, in a cat arching its back in the sun, and in the eyes of *la belle boulangère* in her white apron." For many, this, *the daily ordinary*, is the essence of sacred Paris. As the poet Rilke—not a churchgoer—wrote while he worked in Paris as Rodin's assistant, "I find you God in all things and in all my fellow creatures pulsing with your life." Nature, he called "the landscape of the soul."

Paris memory embraces all these things, the unexpected and hidden presences: we began with the image of van Gogh shouting praise on the hills of Montmartre and then, further on in this book, desiring the sacred in the stars over **Auvers-sur-Oise**. Such ecstasies—of visionaries and artists as well as of travelers—and the music of choirs and trumpets and organs ascending to the roof of **la Madeleine** or **Saint-Sulpice**, their high vaults reverberating with the music of Fauré, Poulenc, or Couperin, to name only a few—this is the legacy of *Sacred Paris,* past and living.

Finding it is the pleasure of this guidebook. And it is the city's greatest gift: *l'amour du vivre,* the love of life.

—Susan Cahill
New York City

ÎLE DE LA CITÉ

Cathedral of Notre-Dame of Paris

CATHEDRAL OF NOTRE-DAME OF PARIS

LOCATION: 6, PARVIS NOTRE-DAME
HOURS: Mon–Sun, 8:00–6:45
MÉTRO: Cité; Hôtel de Ville
www.notredamedeparis.fr

Lovers alone wear sunlight," an American poet wrote.

I last entered *Notre-Dame* on a chilly gray afternoon in November 2018. It had been raining for days. There was no line outside, a rarity on the Parvis. Inside, the aisles were unclogged. I've been inside the cathedral many times since my first long-ago visit to Paris. As I stood now in the Crossing, at my back a statue of *Jeanne d'Arc* on her horse and just next to me the famous statue of the *"Virgin of Paris"*—*"so overpoweringly lovely and inaccessible,"* wrote the architectural critic Allan Temko—*"an Empress of Heaven. . . . She is Notre-Dame of Paris, she was . . . medieval France"*—all of a sudden, on that dull November day, the sun came out. Bright. Electric. Colored light shooting down from the high church's high windows to hit statues and pillars and people.

"*The sapphire I know is there,*" wrote Denise Levertov.

It never crossed my mind that I would not be inside *Notre-Dame* again, would not lay eyes on *la belle mère de Paris* for years.

When you're inside *Notre-Dame,* standing in the Crossing, looking north at the Rose Window—the northern rose, with its stories from the Old Testament—there is sometimes, no matter what the weather outside, a dim light or glow flash flooding blue and rose upon massive gray stone pillars. That line from a poem by—the name now comes to me—*e. e. cummings*: "*Lovers alone wear sunlight.*"

The cathedral, with its high-to-the-sky windows— "medieval blue"—is the love object here. Beauty, the deep blue mother light, now touches the ancient church everywhere, through every window, in every corner, chapel, aisle. *Notre-Dame,* the mother of cathedrals all over Europe. "*Tangled up in blue.*"

Visitors, thirteen million a year, have mixed reactions to the "Virgin's Church." In the stillness, there's a feeling of reverence. You might also sense a ho-hum indifference as you find yourself stuck inside swarms of tourists. "*Disneyland,*" sneered a bearded young man to his partner. Another tourist mecca, an exemplar of mass tourism. "*Skip Notre-Dame, skip the whole Cité,*" my friend Beryl, a child of the Bible Belt, had advised when I was planning my first trip to the City of Light. "*It's Times Square on the Seine.*"

Visitors, most days, line up outside the cathedral on the Parvis, the large plaza in front of it and parallel to the equestrian statue of a heroic Charlemagne (who was, in fact, short, fat, ugly, and illiterate). Once admitted, they shuffle along in the direction of the high altar: distant—east, where in the Middle Ages, the rising sun was believed to offer life to all on this altar table of sacrifice and commemoration. Twelfth-century visitors—1163 was the year of the cathedral's first groundbreaking—had never seen vaults this high. "The Cathedral is pure upward thrust, rising to God, nearly one hundred and ten feet to the main vault," writes *Allan Temko* in his book *Notre-Dame of Paris,* which Lewis Mumford calls "the best introduction I know to help one enjoy what is left of medieval Paris today."

The complicated history of Paris, from the prehistoric past to the present, haunts the cathedral, making it a living theater of horrors and glory. Druids performed human sacrifice here (their altar discovered beneath the cathedral's altar by archaeologists in 1781). Centuries after the pagan druids and then Caesar's Romans disappeared, the kings and queens of early royal families—the Merovingians, the Carolingians, the Capets—having seized the ancient *Île de la Cité* and its prosperous commercial ports for themselves for more than a millennium, considered themselves divine appointees of the gods, or centuries on, the one God whom most early medieval people would come to worship.

For believers, or for pilgrims searching out the beauty of Paris, or for people just wanting to sit down and rest, *Notre-Dame* has always been a sacred destination, a divine presence. Mary, the mother of Jesus, the *Mystical Rose (rosa mystica)* is present. The anonymous thirteenth-century writers of the *Litany of the Blessed Virgin*, perhaps monks from a Paris scriptorium, called her that. They also called her *House of Gold (domus aurea)*, *Morning Star (stella matutina)*, *Virgin most merciful (virgo clemens)*, *Mother most amiable (mater amabilis)* to name a few of her other titles.

The Rose, *rosa mystica*, is everywhere. In the design of the windows, in the sculptured images on the capitals, on the choir stalls and the exterior façades which show scenes from the life of the Virgin. The standard explanation of her church's origin as a *cathedral* is that the word *cathedral* comes from the Latin *"cathedra,"* meaning *"chair"*: the cathedral is the site of the bishop's chair, where he sits in power and judgment. The bishop is the human stand-in for the hierarchical structure of the church. But in *Notre-Dame,* the Rose rules.

Parisians do not deny their mixed-up history: the mix of polarities, the brutal and the safe, the ugliness and tenderness, lights and shadows. *Notre-Dame* is perhaps the most powerful site of the city's mixed collective memory: its double consciousness of love and repulsion, the place where "the historical consciousness of the French people has focused," to quote Colin Jones in *Paris: A Biography of a City.* Without such a mix, the sense of irony that is everywhere in Paris might never have asserted its edgy presence.

It's huge: 65,000 square feet in floor space, 130 meters in total length. The nave is flanked by double aisles; the double ambulatory flanks the five bays of the choir; 37 chapels in honor of 150 saints surround all these spaces. There is so much to look at above ground: high above the nave, light descends from the clerestory windows; the buttresses do seem to fly; visitors study and photograph the small carved details of the choir stalls, tombs, statues. There are devils, snakes, the angelic smiles of saints, acanthus, roses.

Hidden underneath this massive public monument are the layered remains of several earlier sites of worship discovered over the centuries: the fourth-century BC altar of the druids—the priesthood of the Celtic tribes named the *Parisii* by Julius Caesar; the traders, fishermen, and forest creatures who worshipped the water (the Seine was twice as wide then as it is now); a temple from 54 BC, when the Romans arrived, dedicating the temple to Jupiter; the church of *Saint-Étienne* (Stephen, the first martyr), founded in 528, after the Romans left; a smaller church, the Carolingian *Notre-Dame* of the 700s to 800s, built nearest to the Seine on the eastern tip of the Cité behind *Saint-Étienne*'s. The Normans (or Norsemen) invaded and destroyed the city throughout the ninth century, burning down the first *Notre-Dame*; rioters would tear down the episcopal palace on the southwest corner in 1831. The cathedral would always be a target. In time it represented the double power of the Church and the Monarchy. Today's cathedral rises above all these layers of subterranean ruins and myth and horrors.

At times there's a deep quiet here, despite the crowds. People sit and kneel and stand, their heads tilted back to look up into the vaults, at the roof and the blue windows, north, east, south, and west. I remember the character, Lambert Strether, a nineteenth-century visitor from New England, the protagonist of Henry James's novel *The Ambassadors*, sitting alone in the shadows, slightly revolted by all the churchiness. Protestantism—the Puritans—brought none of Catholicism's elaborate architecture across the ocean.

The medieval poet *François Villon*, born 1431 (the year **Jeanne d'Arc** was murdered), a notorious roistering student, thief, jailbird, street fighter, accused murderer of a priest, a famously bawdy and delicately lyric poet, beloved by Blake and Joyce—*"Mais où sont les neiges d'antan"*—*Villon* set many poems here, in what was one of his and his mother's local churches (they lived nearby in the Latin Quarter). The poems include *Ballade for Praying to Our Lady* (written, perhaps, for his destitute and pious mother). A number of the *ballades* ring with a sweet undogmatic faith. *"Our Lord, as such he do I confess / and wish in this faith to live and die."* His trusting faith as well as his delight in the pleasures of the body is the strongest motif in his *Testament*, ripe with sexy jokes and ambiguous puns, an irreverent laughter capturing the low and high life of Paris. Dominant in all his work is sympathy for the poor, for sinners like himself, for the oppressed. His comedy shows his contempt for the oppressors roaming Paris: lawyers, judges, clerical hierarchy. The enemy.

The ideologues of the French Revolution—Robespierre and his disciples—bear not a trace of the likes of Villon. Rigid, cruel, puritanical, their mobs tried to incinerate the Virgin's church. They chopped away from the front façade the sculptured heads of the prophets; they either mistook them for the heads of kings or thought they were all part of a piece; the differences didn't matter. ("Nothing is the same as anything else," wrote Michael Walzer.) *Notre-Dame* was renamed Temple of Reason. Jesus Christ, the nobody from small-town Nazareth, was renamed the Supreme Being. *Rosa mystica* was reidentified as a "goddess," the actress playing her in a triumphal tableau bedecked in red, white, and blue chiffon. The cult of abstraction signaled the stupidity of the regime.

Then came Napoleon, who returned the cathedral to its original Roman Catholic identity—hierarchical, monarchical—as he crowned himself emperor here, stealing the pope's scene and reminding Paris that the cathedral always signified as a site of power. The Virgin's love of the people, the powerless, anonymous poor, belonged to *Notre-Dame*'s identity as a site of mythology, a myth of the Middle Ages that is still embraced. "Marie," said the composer and musician *Francis Poulenc,* "she understands everything."

There was nothing fanciful about the Parisian poor in any era. They were as real as the mud that caked on everything in the medieval streets and then spattered the beggars who were everywhere in the centuries that followed. The Virgin's church sheltered them.

In the early nineteenth century, Victor Hugo made the poor people of Paris the protagonists of his novel *The Hunchback of Notre Dame* (1837). *Quasimodo,* Hugo's misshapen dwarf ("he was born one-eyed, humpbacked, and lame") was the church's bell ringer, who loved the bell *"Marie"* in the south tower. He loved the gypsy *Esmeralda*. Most of all he loved his cathedral, "his egg, his nest, his home, his country, the universe." He was "perpetually subject to its mysterious influence."

Paris rejoiced when the radical Commune of 1871 failed to burn down their church. The fire was set; rescuers from the nearby *Hôtel-Dieu* broke down the doors and put it out. A German bomb hit the cathedral's roof in World War I. *Notre-Dame* escaped the Nazis: Hitler had given the order to mine all religious and historical monuments as well as the bridges of the Seine: he intended to leave the Allies a "smoking ruin" when they came from Normandy to take back Paris in August 1944. The story goes that the German general Dietrich von Choltitz refused to carry out his boss's order: Choltitz, believing that Hitler had gone insane, allowed the mining of the monuments but then refused to order the lighting of the fuses.

These are a few of the historical "miracles" that have saved the life of *Notre-Dame*. The story of her blind organist, *Louis Vierne* (1870–1937), who wrote symphonies for the cathedral's organ, a magnificent *Cavaillé-Coll* instrument, is another point of light along the complex continuum of the church's history. He started out as a student of César Franck and was appointed to the *Notre-Dame* organ in 1901. His recitals were legendary, attracting large and faithful audiences. In 1937, *Vierne* had a heart attack while playing his organ. He died at the keyboard.

Contemporary Paris still gathers here in solidarity to celebrate the survival of church and city. In World War II, Charles de Gaulle led a parade of thousands inside *Notre-Dame* the day after the Liberation (August 25, 1944) to honor the *Virgin, Mater Dei,* and offer thanksgiving for the Liberation. Snipers hidden in the balcony, under the clerestory windows, tried to pick him off, but de Gaulle didn't flinch though his companions dove beneath the kneelers.

These days, Paris comes to sing and remember their deliverance from the latest attacks by the terrorists of 2015.

Fluctuat nec mergitur is the motto of Paris: *She is tossed by the waves but does not drown . . .*

APRIL 15, 2019: 3:45 P.M.
*A friend calls from Paris just as I've typed the words "*Fluctuat nec mergitur.*"*

"Notre-Dame is on fire," she shouts into the phone. We turn on the TV. My husband and I stand openmouthed, horrified. For hours we watch her burn, our eyes stuck on the towers and the north Rose window.

9:45 P.M.
The north window—the Rose—made of the original thirteenth-century glass—has held. And the towers.

President Macron declares the cathedral will be repaired and open to visitors in five years. Parisians gather in front of the smoking ruins until after midnight. Young, old, male, female, many join in singing the "Salve Regina." Many are weeping.

In the months that follow, asbestos and lead from the smoldering cathedral blow poison over the Île de la Cité, its schools and bridges and apartments, the bistros and gardens. The repairs are going slowly. Liturgies are being held in **Saint-Germain l'Auxerrois** *(see p. 127).*

DECEMBER 24, 2019, "THERE WILL BE NO CHRISTMAS AT NOTRE-DAME"

From the New York Times:

> *[I]t is terribly sad for anyone who has ever been to Paris in winter. . . . It is a reminder of how great an emptiness the fire left in the heart of Paris and far beyond. Notre-Dame is more than a church, . . . more even than a symbol of one of the great cities of the world. Like many of the earth's great cultural landmarks, it has a life of its own; it is a living character in art, literature, music and legend, and a place where a tired passer-by can drop in for some rest and quiet thought. It carries a message that every visitor can interpret in his or her own way.*

MARCH 12, 2020

Now Charles de Gaulle Airport is closed because of the Covid-19 pandemic. No one knows for how long. **Notre-Dame** *is still standing; the repairs continue.*

Paris does not drown.

Nearby

ÎLE SAINT-LOUIS: **Place Louis Aragon.** *The western tip of the* **Île Saint-Louis.** *Cross the bridge between the eastern tip of the* **Île de la Cité** *and the west end of* **the Île Saint-Louis.** *Take a short left to* **Place Louis Aragon.** *Look west, over one of the city's* *loveliest views of the* **Seine**. *"Paris is the Seine," the local saying goes. The surrealist poet* **Louis Aragon** *(1897–1982) lived on the île when he wrote the novel* Aurélien: *the Seine is a main character. A Communist, editor, essayist, member of the Académie Goncourt, Aragon was the* **résistant** *most hunted by the Gestapo during the Occupation.*

ROBERT BRESSON (1901–1999): *lived above the* **Place Louis Aragon** *at number 49, fifth floor. With Jean-Luc Godard, Bresson is considered France's greatest filmmaker. "There is the feeling that God is everywhere," he said in 1973, "and the more I live, the more I see that in nature, in the country. When I see a tree, I see that God exists. I try to catch and to convey the idea that we have a soul and that the soul is in contact with God. That's the first thing I want to get in my films." These include* Diary of a Country Priest *(based on Georges Bernanos's novel of the same title)*, L'Argent (The Money), Pickpocket, A Man Escaped, *and* Au Hasard Balthazar.

COLLÈGE DES BERNARDINS: *Leave the Île de la Cité, cross to the Left Bank on the Pont de l'Archevêché, turn left, walk east on the Quai de Montebello to the Quai de la Tournelle; turn right on* **rue de Poissy, into no. 20. From the Île Saint-Louis, cross to the Left Bank on the Pont de la Tournelle, then turn right on the rue de Poissy. (Open Mon–Sat, 10–6; Sun and hols, 2–6; closed Aug and Christmas)**. *Founded in 1244, this Cistercian monastery, restored in 2008, is now part of the Cathedral School, a center for lectures, classes, research, concerts, and festivals. A magnificent large nave greets you on entrance. There's a guided tour at www.collegedesberdardines.fr.*

Related Readings

Louis Aragon, *Aurélien,* 2 vols., trans. Eithne Wilkins. Ranked 51 in *Le Monde*'s 100 Best Books of the Century.

Rollin Smith, *Louis Vierne: Organist of Notre-Dame Cathedral*

Victor Hugo, *The Hunchback of Notre-Dame*

Robert Bresson, *Notes on the Cinematographer*

Sainte-Chapelle

SAINTE-CHAPELLE

LOCATION: 8, BOULEVARD DU PALAIS
HOURS: Daily, Mar–Oct, 9:30–6; Nov–Feb, 9–5
MÉTRO: Cité; Saint-Michel
PARISPASS.COM/PARIS-ATTRACTIONS/SAINTE
   -CHAPELLE.HTML

S*ainte-Chapelle* may be the popular favorite of all the holy places in Paris. In every season, Parisians and travelers join the queue on the *boulevard du Palais* near the corner of *Pont Saint-Michel* and a three-minute walk west of Notre-Dame. Sunshine is an absolute necessity for this visit.

The memory of the place never fades. On first sight, its beauty stuns. The blending of the colors of the stained glass windows in the upper chapel (*chapelle haute*)—predominantly tones of deep blue and red—their lights ascend into the high air as if the air itself is moving into another realm. The stained glass represents the jeweled walls of heaven described in the Bible. In medieval theology, light signifies the presence of the divine. The radiant church windows, for believers, are an image of heaven on earth.

King Louis IX (reigned 1214–1270) had the chapel built as a shrine to hold the relics of Christ's crown of thorns and some fragments of the true cross which he bought in Constantinople (1239) during the Crusades in the Middle East. He planned to turn Paris into a new *locus sanctus* equal to the holy city of Rome, the original sacred ground of Christianity's ancient treasure. It took less than ten years (1242–1248) for the chapel to be completed, thanks to the genius of the master builder (probably Pierre de Montreuil, who also worked on Saint-Denis, Notre-Dame, and Saint-Germain-des-Prés) as well as his fellow artisans, the stonemasons, iron workers, goldsmiths, and most especially the stained glass artists.

The relics were hidden deep in a golden shrine under a wooden canopy in the apse; the king showed them to the faithful every year on Good Friday. Damaged during the Revolution of 1789—the gold of the reliquary was melted down—the relics were transferred to the treasury of Notre-Dame Cathedral until the fire of April 15, 2019—when they were again transferred to safety.

The walls of the upper chapel are covered with fifteen stained glass windows (cleaned and restored in 2008) that show some of the stories from the Hebrew and Christian Bibles. (In the lower chapel you can pick up guides that map the locations of the depicted scenes.) An iconographic scheme shows at top center the Passion of Christ, flanked on the left (as you face it from the nave) by the childhood of Christ and on the right by the life of John the Baptist and the Book of Daniel. Along the left and right sides you can see, to name a few, scenes from Genesis; the Books of Joshua, Isaiah, and Kings; and scenes from the stories of Judith and Job. The last window on the right shows Louis himself, dressed as a penitent, carrying the sacred relics on foot to Paris. At the west end of the chapel you see the Rose window with its eighty-six panels from the Apocalypse. Twelve life-size painted statues of the apostles stand on twelve pillars in front of the windows. (Binoculars are useful.)

The sparkling prophets and poets, martyrs and saints figure as the main characters of the Western religious tradition in medieval France. Inside the nave and high up beyond the tracery and quatrefoils, the images of the West's sacred heroes shine forth.

The crypt-like lower chapel (*chapelle basse*)—the narrow staircase at the rear of *chapelle haute*—is painted with golden fleurs-de-lys, symbols of France, on a blue background; the towers of Castile, emblem of Blanche of Castile, are painted on a red surface. The lower chapel, its shadowy vaults and columns supporting the upper chapel, served in the Middle Ages as the parish church for the servants, soldiers, and courtiers; the staircase leads upstairs to the resplendent church reserved for the royal family and their guests. These days the lower vaults function as vendors' stalls where medieval tchotchkes are sold to tourists.

The two-story composition of **Sainte-Chapelle** reflected the hierarchical identity of Louis IX's kingdom: the church and the monarchy, upstairs; the lower church for the laity and the servants. Perhaps this doubleness can also be read as analogous to the legacy of opposites we read in King Louis's biography.

He was the only French king to be canonized. The pope honored Louis more for his faithful politics than his legendary piety.

Louis IX was well-known for his activism on behalf of the poor, the lepers, the blind, and prostitutes. He washed the feet of his nobles. He listened to the complaints of ordinary people and tried to enact justice. He prayed and fasted and heard several masses throughout each day. Such commitment to religious practices and to a social justice based in Scripture was rare among kings.

But Saint/King Louis also obeyed with a degree of subservience more common to a slave or slave master. In compliance with the rules of a hierarchical Church and the commands of the papal throne, he established the Inquisition, the centuries-long policy of imprisonment, torture, and murder of so-called heretics and dissidents. He ordered the expulsion of the Jews from the Left Bank and eventually in 1254 from France. It wasn't only that, like his grandfather Phillip Augustus (1165–1223), he coveted the Jews' wealth and property. For Louis, their sin was a refusal to acknowledge and venerate the virginity of Mary, the mother of Christ. In the southwest, he ordered the torture and extinction of the Albigensian heretics who also rejected various dogmas of Catholicism.

Obeying Pope Gregory IX, he oversaw the public burning of twelve thousand volumes of the Talmud, each volume having been copied laboriously by hand. King Louis was the only Christian monarch to obey the pope's order to destroy the Talmud. The majestic king had an obedient soul. In northeastern Paris (now the neighborhood of Belleville), he erected the notorious gibbet of Montfaucon where heretics and criminals were tortured and murdered, their corpses hung for years to rot as feast for wolves, rats, and dogs. Perhaps most infamous was his order that Jews mark their clothing with a circle, square, or star of red or yellow fabric, a degradation that, as the world knows, had staying power into the Nazi era of the twentieth century. (See "Louis IX, The Dark Side of Sainthood," pages 18–24 in *The Streets of Paris*.)

He was a passionate Crusader, his mission the destruction of Muslim infidels in the East.

The French historian Maurice Druon in *The History of Paris from Caesar to Saint Louis,* along with other historians, identifies Louis's fanatic mother as the progenitor of Louis's sadism and twisted religious manias: He "was one of the great neurotics of history," writes Druon. "Had he not inclined to saintliness he might have been a monster. Neros are made of the same fibre. . . ." Queen Mother Blanche taught young Louis to fear the devil—who is everywhere—by mortifying his body round the clock, with time out on the back stairs between his and his wife's bedchambers. Dutifully, they conceived eleven children.

Louis IX was and remains beloved in the memory of Paris. His image and his crown are carved on statues and painted into the stained glass of churches. He is depicted smiling gently over his people, feeding the beggars, staring in blank sanctity.

His thirteenth-century almsgiving, conjoined with his pious cruelty, has little in common with the ethos of the preceding twelfth century, the period of the true French Renaissance when the leaders of Church policy had, in the words of Alistair Horne, "little difficulty in squaring love of God with love of worldly beauty and of the sensuous world"; the people of God had looked on Gothic beauty, heard sermons presenting a theology of light. The twelfth-century Christ and his messengers preached the lilies of the field and the birds of the air, the indiscriminate falling of rain and sunlight on all people.

In Louis's thirteenth century, the themes of church preaching shifted to sin and the omnipresence of Satan. Obeying his pope, Louis ordered his Crusades (1248–1254; 1270); the Inquisition; his new university, the Sorbonne, as rigid and dogmatic as its namesake, Louis's confessor, Robert de Sorbon. A century later that faculty would advocate the public burning of the nineteen-year-old heretic Joan of Arc.

In the time of Blanche and Louis IX, the Christian religion changed radically. But *Saint-Chapelle* remains. And this sacred place was also Louis's idea. It's the same place today as it was in the dawn light when Louis knelt at morning Mass.

In the evening, queues for tickets to **Sainte Chapelle** concerts on the sidewalk of *boulevard du Palais* are long in high season. Inside, as you sit and wait, there's time to contemplate the enigmas of history, the opposites beyond resolution. Then, in a surround of Bach and Mozart and the architecture of jeweled radiance, history gets lost in space.

Nearby

THE CONCIERGERIE: *Enter at the north end of **boulevard du Palais**. Same times as for **Sainte-Chapelle**. Conciergerie .monuments-nationaux.fr. The most moving place inside this huge prison on the site of ancient palaces is the area of the **cell and chapel of Marie-Antoinette**, the scapegoated wife and queen of King Louis XVI. She was charged as a sexual pervert; gambler; and a spendthrift, callous royal. She was guillotined on October 16, 1793. Fifty years later she was quoted as saying of the starving peasants,* "Qu'ils mangent de la brioche" *(Let them eat brioche), which she did not say.*

HENRI IV ON THE PONT NEUF: *Good King Henri Quatre sits high on the equestrian statue on the **Pont Neuf**, the oldest bridge in Paris, at the tip of the Île de la Cité, connecting Quai du Louvre and the Quai des Grands Augustins. The bridge was designed so that the king could travel between the Louvre, where he lived, and **Notre-Dame** and the **Abbey of Saint-Germain-des-Prés** (see p. 77). Henri was one of France's most beloved kings, but not for his piety or militant crusading. His religion, as he put it, belonged to those* "who honestly follow their conscience . . . I belong to the faith of all those who are gallant and good." *Bap-*

tized Catholic, raised Protestant, he returned to Catholicism to end the civil Wars of Religion between the two sects and to take the throne *(1589–1610)* he had inherited. No inquisitor, he was a pluralist to the bone, telling Parliament, *"We should not make any distinction between Catholics and Huguenots—we should all be good Frenchmen."* Beauty was more sacred to Henri Quatre's new city than any church dogma. He was later assassinated by a fanatical Catholic.

Henri IV has always been remembered as the randy, charming sensualist with many mistresses and children, who made war-ravaged Paris beautiful: **Place des Vosges**; the completion of the **Pont Neuf**; the **extension of the Louvre; Place Dauphine**, just east across the bridge, built for his son Louis XIII. (For more about Henri's Paris, see The Streets of Paris, *pp. 37–47.)* The Vedettes du Pont Neuf are sightseeing barges that leave from here, alongside **Square du Vert-Galant** *(see* Hidden Gardens of Paris, *p. 3, and **Vedettesdupontneuf.com**).*

LA TAVERNE HENRI IV—*13, PLACE DU PONT NEUF. TEL: 01 43 54 27 90. Every day except Sunday, noon to 3; 7–12:30. A small wine bar that feels ancient, serving delicious charcuterie, tartines.* "The archetype of the great bistro à vin," *writes the* New York Times. *On the western tip of **Place Dauphine** just across from Henri IV's statue on the Pont Neuf.*

MUSÉE DU CLUNY/MUSÉE NATIONAL DU MOYEN ÂGE: *The greatest attraction is the series of six medieval tapestries,* **The Lady and the Unicorn**. *The newly restored museum—at 6, Place Paul Painlevé, off boulevard Saint-Germain, open Weds–Mon, 9–5:45—has a very good bookstore though it's not as comprehensive as the old one: make sure you pick up* "The Lady and the Unicorn," *a folding guide by Jean-Patrice Boudet. The best I've read: it comments clearly and provocatively on* *the meaning of the enigmatic tapestries. Do the tapestries glorify the heart or the intellect? Both? "It's a polyphonic work of art," writes Boudet.*

Related Readings

Colin Jones, *Paris: The Biography of a City*

Desmond Seward, *The First Bourbon: Henri IV of France and Navarre*

Robert Chazan, in *The Trial of the Talmud: Paris, 1240*

THE LEFT BANK

Saint-Séverin

The Latin Quarter

SAINT-SÉVERIN

LOCATION: 3, RUE DES PRÊTRES SAINT-SÉVERIN
HOURS OF MASSES: Mon–Fri, 12:15, 7; Sat, 12:15; Sun, 10:30
MÉTRO: Cité; Saint-Michel; Cluny-La Sorbonne

Knots of tourists, shoppers—and their hawkers—choke the narrow cobbled streets winding around this part of the Latin Quarter. The warren of streets goes back to the city's beginnings: *rue de la Huchette, rue Xavier Privas, rue du Chat-qui-Pêche. Saint-Séverin* on *rue des Prêtres Saint-Séverin* stands its ancient sacred ground. At most hours of the day there is a stillness inside the church and along *rue des Prêtres Saint-Séverin,* where you'll find the front entrance.

The *Saint-Séverin quartier* began as a place of worship in the early fifth century. The hermit Servinus—*Séverin*—lived on the nearby banks of the Seine. When he died, a small Romanesque chapel was built on his tomb site. Or so the story goes. Centuries later, in 1253, with the Sorbonne digging in up the hill of *rue Saint-Jacques* and the students coming downhill to crowd into the new *Saint-Séverin* for Mass, the church was enlarged again and again (and repaired after periodic fires). To accommodate the increasing numbers of churchgoers in the thirteenth, fourteenth, and fifteenth centuries, side chapels and more aisles were added, the nave widened. This church is not symmetrical. In the seventeenth century the church was completely altered; more gargoyles and flying buttresses appeared on the exterior. A sacristan or a priest will unlock the door to the south side where the galleries of a fifteenth-century charnel house, the only one surviving in Paris, still survives; in the garden you'll see a small ancient statue of a monk.

The stained glass windows (some from *Saint-Germain des Prés*), tell the ancient Bible stories. Their colors are not only red and blue; there's a deep green foliage and brilliant ruby between the images. In the rear of the church as you enter, in a chapel on the left, there's an image of Saint Vincent de Paul caring for the poor and baptizing a baby outside in *rue de la Huchette*.

Shafts of stone spiral around a double central column, bursting into leaf at the top as if the column were a palm tree. Over the years statues were added to the side chapels: Saint Francis of Assisi, Saint Thérèse of Lisieux (whom Édith Piaf loved, wearing her medal from when she was four years old into her grave at the age of forty-eight). The organ of 1745—played by *Camille Saint-Saëns* and *Gabriel Fauré*—is still one of the city's finest, at the center of *Saint-Séverin's Sacred Music repertoire* performed in Paris.

In the twentieth century, stained glass windows were added to the first level, beneath the old traditional windows: seven of them, abstract patterns (by Jean Bazaine, 1966), signify the seven sacraments flashing wild flames of light. High above, the ribbed vaulting gives the nave and double ambulatories a dramatic cover. One look and you understand the art historian's phrase: *Flamboyant Gothic*.

The small chapel in the southeast corner of the church, designed by the royal architect *Jules Hardouin-Mansart* in 1673, is called variously the "Mansart Chapel," the "Chapel of the Holy Sacrament," and the "Holy Communion Chapel." Mass is celebrated here every day at 12:15, attended by workers, students, ordinary Parisians. Strangers like myself. The room is small and intimate. The appointments: tabernacle; altar—a rectangular stone slab that looks as if it could have been carved by druid priests (or Celtic *Parisii*) who worshipped the nearby *Seine*; a modern crucifix on the wall above the tabernacle. Each bronze object has a simplicity and grace that rings true to the story being commemorated. Also on the wall above the stone altar is a painting of Christ and two friends at *Emmaus* (see p. 54).

Along the rear wall, beneath the yellow glass windows, you see a dozen or so framed lithographs of the Passion—the *Miserere*—the work of *Georges Rouault* (1871–1958), who grew up poor in Belleville and was trained as a painter by Gustave Moreau and, inspired by French medieval masters, as a maker of stained glass. The series commemorates Rouault's father's death and Psalm 50. Each one has a dark cast, registering a "static accepted suffering." In the words of John Berger in *About Looking*: "*Rouault*'s work is not conventional religious art, nor is it Catholic propaganda." The lithographs will stop you in your tracks.

I visit this church when I'm in Paris. "*There's something about Saint-Séverin*," a friend who once lived in the *quartier* told me.

There is the beauty. Strange. Ancient. Modern. The centuries haunt the air, the stories of faith and desire. There is a story about the Mansart Chapel having been built to counter the influence of bleak puritanical Jansenism in seventeenth-century Paris. *Saint-Séverin* is a kind of rebuttal, expressing joy and color versus a religion haunted by sin. (See the story of *Saint-Médard*, p. 59, about ten minutes away.)

* * *

There is also *Saint-Séverin*'s mostly unknown history as a witness to French courage. The Society of Jesus (the religious order known as the Jesuits) organized and assembled here many young university students (the JEC, the Young Christian Students) in the 1930s to resist Nazi hatred: *"A Frenchman who remained unmoved by a Jewish countryman suffering under present conditions would not be a Christian,"* as Professor/*Père* Yves de Montcheuil put it. Père Michel Riquet, who in the thirties had rescued and hidden anti-fascist refugees from Austria and Spain in Paris, told the students gathered in *Saint-Séverin*:

> *My brothers, if you want to know what conduct to adopt during these dark times, go and read the words on the plinth of the statue of Danton at Saint-Germain-des-Prés. "To overcome the enemies of the fatherland, you must dare, dare again, and forever dare."*

Père Riquet was captured by the Nazis and sent to Dachau and then Mauthausen where he was remembered by survivors and historians as a model of extraordinary courage.

> *We are made of history. We live in history the way fish live in water. Whether we know it or not, we are made of it.*

I read this passage one noontime sitting in the *Mansart Chapel*, in that day's book review in the *New York Times International Edition*. I was thinking about the anonymous *résistants* of *Saint-Séverin,* wondering what had happened to them and their mostly anonymous professors/priests. There is a bronze sculpture commemorating them inside the *rue de Vaugirard* entrance to *Le Jardin du Luxembourg,* near the *Medici Fountain*.

DIRECTIONS: Walk south from **Saint-Séverin** to boulevard Saint-Germain, then right, then left and up boulevard Saint-Michel to the rue de Vaugirard entrance to the Luxembourg.

The French philosopher, *résistante*, and political activist **Simone Weil,** a product of the great Parisian schools of this *quartier,* also hid Austrians and Germans fleeing the Nazis in the thirties. She undoubtedly knew **Saint-Séverin** and the anti-Nazi activism of the French students and the Jesuits. Born Jewish and raised in a secular family, she developed a devotion to religion as an adult, visiting many Parisian churches but with no interest in receiving the sacrament of baptism or joining the Church, which she called *"that great totalitarian beast with an irreducible kernel of truth."* (Though she loved the liturgy and some Catholic theology, she hated the church's historical record of Inquisition, Crusades, and *"let him be anathema."*) In an essay, "Forms of the Implicit Love of God," she writes about the love of *"the beauty of the world,"* which she saw everywhere in Paris:

> *At the present time . . . the beauty of the world is almost the only way by which we can allow God to penetrate us. . . . The beauty of the world is . . . the most natural way of approach . . . the trap God most frequently uses in order to win [a soul] and open it to the breath from on high.*

A *résistante* after *1933,* when Hitler came to power, she died before the Liberation. Albert Camus, an editor at Gallimard, published her writings posthumously in the forties and fifties, calling her *"the only great spirit of our time."* T. S. Eliot agreed: she was *"a woman of genius, of a kind of genius akin to that of the saints."*

DIRECTIONS: She lived at *3, rue Auguste Comte*, marked with a plaque. Walk from north to south through the *Luxembourg*, where she often walked with a friend after classes at the Sorbonne; exit through the southern entrance, bearing right.

If you exit *Saint-Séverin* through its rear door, you find yourself on the ancient *rue Saint-Jacques*, crowded with tourists here, so close to the *Seine*; but as you climb the hill, heading south, the crowds thin and you can see many ancient buildings before you reach the top and the churches of *Saint-Étienne-du-Mont* and *Val-de-Grâce*.

Nearby

SAINT-JULIEN-LE-PAUVRE: *Right around the corner from Shakespeare and Company, on* **rue Saint-Julien le Pauvre**, *the church, one of the first sanctuaries on the* **Left Bank**, *erected in the sixth century, became one of the important churches of the Sorbonne where Saint Thomas Aquinas, Dante, François Villon, and Rabelais prayed. The simplicity of the current church, now Greek Orthodox, is lovely, with a striking iconostasis, a screen with icons separating the chancel from the nave. The church offers classical concerts at night, but these days, the church is not open during the day. On the north side of the church,* **Square René Viviani**, *a friendly square with a view of* **Notre-Dame**, *is a good place to pass the time while you wait for the church doors to open—perhaps reading Flaubert's religious story (unusual for him), "The Legend of Saint Julian the Hospitaller," in his* Three Tales. *The words and images on the central fountain in the square are taken from the story. Julian killed his parents but wound up a beloved saint.*

THE ABBEY BOOKSHOP: *Exiting **Saint-Séverin** by the front door, turn left, walk half a block until you come to **rue de la Parcheminerie;** turn right and stop into **no. 29,** Brian Spence's shop. Originally **rue des Écrivains** in 1273, named for the scribes who were the heart of the book trade, it's now the home of bookbinders and illustrators. The shop's owner is hospitable and knows his inventory: he can find anything. Don't hesitate to move inside and look for yourself. I have found treasure (in 2019, a first edition of Charles Péguy's* Basic Verities *translated by Anne and Julian Green, 1943).*

SHAKESPEARE AND COMPANY: *37, **rue de la Bûcherie,** 10–11, seven days. An English-language bookshop packed with customers and books, named in honor of the original shop in **rue de l'Odéon** where owner and publisher Sylvia Beach published James Joyce's* Ulysses *in 1922. A fun place on Bloomsday, June 16, with readings and wine tasting. Books about Paris, French writers, and a new café next door.*

Related Reading

Gustave Flaubert, "The Legend of Saint Julian the Hospitaller," in *Three Tales*

Julian Green, "St Julian the Poor," in *Paris*

Emmanuel Carrère, *The Kingdom*

Simone Weil, *Waiting for God*

Saint-Étienne-du-Mont

SAINT-ÉTIENNE-DU-MONT

LOCATION: PLACE SAINTE-GENEVIÈVE ON MONT SAINTE-
GENÈVIEVE
HOURS: Tues–Fri, 8:45–7:45; Sat–Sun, 8:45–12 and
2–7:45; closed Mon
MÉTRO: Maubert-Mutualité
WWW.SAINTETIENNEDUMONT.FR

*The climb up the hill of the cobbled **rue de la Montagne
Sainte-Geneviève** from **rue des Écoles** to the highest spot
in the Latin Quarter can feel like a hard trek to long ago
and faraway. The resonance of centuries and characters
on **Place Sainte-Geneviève** stirs a sense of history as you
move across the wide-open square of the pretty church—
Saint-Étienne-du-Mont—framed by the monumental
Panthéon and the **Bibliothèque Sainte-Geneviève**. People walked here when the settlement was still called by its
Roman name, **Lutetia;** the mountaintop itself was called
Mount Leucotilius.*

Clovis (466–511), king of the Franks (or German
tribes)—who converted to Christianity under the influence of Saint Geneviève—and his wife, Saint Clotilde,
built the original church on this site—as an abbey—after the
occupying Romans had moved on. They named it the basilica of the Holy Apostles. All three were buried here: the
two saintly women and the murderous Merovingian assas-
sin Clovis. ("Clovis managed to kill off most of his family,"

according to Alistair Horne. "After each killing he built a church. He was a great church-builder.")

In the thirteenth century, the pope allowed the Bishop of Paris, Eudes de Sully, to build a larger church, adjoining the abbey church. This one was named Saint Stephen—*Saint Étienne*—for the first Christian martyr.

By the end of the fifteenth century, the church had become too small for the growing student population from the Sorbonne. So it was enlarged and rebuilt between 1492 and 1626, its multiple styles no doubt the result of the many quarrels and conflicting architectural tastes of the abbots of Saint-Geneviève.

Many years later, the religious history of Clovis was of paramount importance to *Charles de Gaulle*. He dated the birth of France to the year when Clovis was baptized. De Gaulle said:

> *For me, the history of France begins with Clovis, who was chosen as King of France by the tribe of Franks, who gave their name to France. Before Clovis, we have the Gallo-Roman and Gaulish history. The deciding element for me is that Clovis was the first king to be baptized a Christian. Mine is a Christian country and I count the history of France from the accession of a Christian king who bore the name of the Franks.*

(On the façade of the cathedral at Reims where the first royal baptism took place, you'll see an image of the sculpted stone barrel—the baptismal font—in which Clovis, whose hair and beard fell to his waist, was pushed down into the cold water on Christmas day 508, wrapped, knotted, as if swaddled in body hair, as Francia became the first Christian kingdom in the West.)

Throughout de Gaulle's life, patriotism and religion were a sacred blend, a kind of mystical marriage. It was as if he had sworn a vow of loyalty to each: Church and Monarchy.

But since de Gaulle—as well as long before de Gaulle—there has been a divorce. France—the Paris this book is looking at—has left behind its Christian marriage. Paris is no longer a Christian city.

And yet friends shout as they argue: *You're wrong! France is always and forever Christian.* Some of these friends are not, or are no longer, Christians themselves. What can't be argued is that Paris was once profoundly Christian, and those roots still reverberate. Socialism, for instance, is a radically Christian form of government. It comes out of the gospels.

Geneviève, independent minded, a woman of conscience and bravery, is the soul of this ancient hill. Her life story is wrapped in mystery, a few facts, dramatic legends. She is honored as the patron saint of Paris, the heroine of French history. Statues of Saint Geneviève show her holding keys: Paris is her spiritual kingdom. She is cherished as the woman who gave France its spine. As a fifteen-year-old girl enclosed in a convent, she taught the French to fight back against tyrants. When Attila the Hun (406–453), of the most savage of the barbarian tribes (which included the Huns, Visigoths, Ostrogoths, Alans, and others), was said to be on his way to slaughter and conquer Paris, Geneviève had a vision. She preached to the people: *"Get down on your knees and pray! I know it, I see it. The Huns will not come."*

Attila, *"flagellum Dei," the scourge of God,* turned back. Geneviève's vision and her intercession with the people of Paris were considered miracles. She was perceived as the heroine who embodied and passed on the spirit of resistance that would inspire the French over the course of many centuries: fighting back (except when she didn't) became her foreign policy, taking on the assaults of despots, taxes, poverty, injustice. Her actions—and her successes—in the face of continued barbaric invasions gave Paris its reputation as "a city protected by God." Her resistance gave the hill its name: *Montagne Sainte-Geneviève*. She lived to be ninety years old. Before and after her death, she (and later her bones) were called on to save the city as more barbaric hordes traveled the Rhine and the Seine to threaten the city. On her feast day, January 3, her relics were paraded in procession around the city, up and down the hill to *Notre-Dame* and back. Her relics, the city believed, and the memory of the courageous woman strengthened Paris to overcome fears of war, epidemic, starvation, drought, and always another invasion. The relics, housed in the church, attracted pilgrims in all seasons, inspiring a devotion at once patriotic and religious in the model of de Gaulle's conscience.

The fifth-century basilica was renamed for her, enlarged: the *Sainte-Geneviève Abbey*, later rechristened *Saint-Étienne-du-Mont*, added more buildings—*la tour Clovis*, which still dominates the hill—the refectories, cloisters, and chapels, only fragments of which remain on the grounds, and buildings of today's *Lycée Henri IV*, each place built or rebuilt on the site of the old abbey.

In 1744 King Louis XV replaced the old church with the grand monument/church of *Sainte-Geneviève*; it was renamed the *Panthéon* at the end of the century after it was secularized at the Revolution (1789–1799). During the Terror (1793) the bones of Saint Geneviève were burned in the *Place de Grève* (now the plaza of the Hôtel de Ville on the Right Bank), her ashes dumped in the Seine. Her tomb was left empty. What had been her church became the property of the secular State; Paris now dedicated the ***Panthéon aux Grands Hommes la Patrie Reconnaissante***: "To the Glory of Great Men." But affection for the city's patron saint remained: huge murals depicting Geneviève's works of social justice decorate the interior. In one, she is watching over her city with an affecting calm, offering bread to hungry Parisians. It's her story that catches your eye as you enter the cold classical tomb.

And still clear in the memory of Paris, there is that cold December day in 1964 when the ashes of ***Jean Moulin,*** the hero of the French Resistance—"the Face of France" in André Malraux's words—were placed in the ***Panthéon*** (he'd been murdered in 1943). In May 2015, the State added to the crypt the remains of four more *résistants*: ***Germaine Tillion, Geneviève de Gaulle-Anthonioz, Pierre Brossolette,*** and ***Jean Zay.*** Finally, there was one feminist writer whom Robespierre himself had sentenced to death during the Terror: ***Olympe de Gouges.*** Each of them had died for their service to the tradition of ***Saint Geneviève***: fighting back.

Inside the present-day church of ***Saint-Étienne-du-Mont,*** it's the vastness that strikes you first. And then a clutter of fantastic fixtures and designs from different historic periods—Romanesque, early Gothic (when Peter Abelard taught in the nearby abbey), Flamboyant Gothic, early and late Renaissance, touches of Baroque. (All those quarreling abbots left their tastes intact.) It's a "*jolly hybrid,*" said one writer, a "*hodgepodge,*" said another.

Most striking to my eyes is the Renaissance jube, or rood screen, the only one left in Paris. Then the spiral stairways at either side of the balustrade. The Gothic ribbed vaulting. The elegant gallery that joins the pillars of the nave and choir. The ambulatory, gloomy, spacious with ribbed vaulting. The wooden pulpit, ornately and superbly carved, covered with reliefs. Stained glass from 1550 in the high nave windows. The high choir windows.

On bright days, light pours in; the organist practices for tonight's concert. Bach's Preludes.

Nearby

BIBLIOTHÈQUE SAINTE-GENEVIÈVE: *Open Sept–June, 10–6; July–Aug, 1–6. www.bsg.univ-paris3.fr. On the northeast side of the **Place Sainte-Geneviève**, to your left as you stand in front of the Panthéon. The great French architect **Henri Labrouste** designed the library—his masterpiece—in the mid-nineteenth century, replacing the five-hundred-year-old one where Ignatius Loyola, the Catholic founder of the Jesuits; John Calvin the Protestant reformer; and Erasmus the Dutch humanist had all studied as students from the nearby theological Collège de Montaigu. In the entrance hall, guides will escort you up the stairs and answer your questions with intelligence and humor. "This is just about the perfect French building," to quote the British travel writer Ian Nairn.*

Rich in silence, of exquisite beauty, the reading room on the second floor is open to visitors. You may sit and read if you're not stunned into stupefaction by the surroundings. You are sitting beneath the famous iron and glass roof, like a curving and beautifully designed skylight above a long double-vaulted aisle: this is one of the most splendid sights in Paris. The library holds a large collection of ancient manuscripts as well as original manuscripts of Baudelaire, Verlaine, Rimbaud, Gide, and Valéry. The impoverished Polish girl Marie Skłodowska, later Madame Curie, studied in this room every night until midnight because it was gas heated, which her flat was not. She said she loved the atmosphere of concentration.

In Italy, libraries are considered sacred spaces. In Paris, too, in this room, there is a sense of contemplation, of research pursued as if it were a holy rite and the thousands of volumes on the shelves a kind of holy scripture. The building occupies the site of the library of the **Abbaye Sainte-Geneviève**, where Peter Abelard dazzled students in the twelfth century. The exterior façade, like a Renaissance palace, is covered with the incised names of the authors who have shaped the sensibility of Europe: Abelard, directly above the front door, Mahoamet, Petrarch, Dante, Chaucer, Bruno, Cervantes, Spinoza, Rabelais, Luther, Vico, to name only a few. No women made the cut.

(If you are thrilled by Labrouste's use of new materials—iron, glass, and light—in his pioneering construction on **Montagne Sainte-Geneviève**, you will also find his other masterpiece on the Right Bank's **rue Richelieu**, no. 58: **the Bibliothèque nationale, site Richelieu**, the main reading room, a place of splendor. Hours: Mon–Fri, 9–5, www.bnf.fr/en/richelieu.)

Related Reading

Julian Jackson, *De Gaulle*

Alistair Horne, *Seven Ages of Paris*

Patrick Marnham, *Resistance and Betrayal: The Death and Life of the Greatest Hero of the French Resistance*

Val-de-Grâce

VAL-DE-GRÂCE

LOCATION: 277, RUE SAINT-JACQUES; 1, PLACE
ALPHONSE LAVERAN

HOURS: Noon–6; closed Mon and Fri; Aug 1, Jan 1,
May 25

MÉTRO: RER B to Port-Royal

WWW.ECOLE-VALDEGRACE.SANTE.DEFENSE.GOUV.FR
/L-EGLISE/EGLISE-DU-VAL-DE-GRACE

DIRECTIONS: Exit métro at Port-Royal, turn left into rue
Henri Barbusse, then right into rue de Val-de-Grâce.
Straight ahead you see the golden dome of the church
of Val-de-Grâce. Or you can walk up the hill of rue
Saint-Jacques, from the end of the Petit Pont.

The golden dome of *Notre-Dame du Val-de-Grâce* rises behind the church at the crest of the ancient *rue Saint-Jacques*. From a distance (or from the top of Tour Montparnasse), it's easy to confuse the dome of Val-de-Grâce with the domes of Les Invalides or the Panthéon, each a gleaming landmark of pride and centuries-old splendor.

Rue Saint-Jacques, in Roman times the Via Superior and the main road south to Orléans from the Île de la Cité, is still the sacred pilgrimage route to Santiago de Compostela, the shrine of Saint James (Saint Jacques) in Spain. Rue Saint-Jacques still links the Latin Quarter with Montparnasse to the south and at the north end the Île de la Cité; on the Right Bank the rue Saint-Jacques changes its name to rue Saint-Martin. The side streets off rue Saint-Jacques are still rich in schools, churches, libraries, commerce, and historical monuments. After the Romans left Lutetia, the traffic of religion dominated the area; it was called "a monastic city." The streets showed signposts of early Christianity's solidarity with the needs of the poor. Many have written that the socialism of France is rooted in its original Christianity.

The seventeenth-century church of *Val-de-Grâce,* in its present Renaissance/Baroque glory, was a latecomer to the hill, built to celebrate the birth of Louis XIV, the Sun King (reigned 1643–1715), son of Louis XIII and Anne of Austria. (It signified, too, like many of the golden domes, the Counter-Reformation triumph of Monarchy and Catholicism over puritanical Protestants.) Louis XIV's parents had been childless for twenty-three years. The designated architects built the church—in his honor—within the walls of a Benedictine convent that was built originally on the ancient royal abbey of Val-de-Grâce. It was one of the many convents Queen Anne had founded in her childless years and where she had spent much of her time: no one liked her at court because she was a foreigner, so she found comfort in the monastery. Thanks to her, Carmelites, Ursulines, the Feuillantines, among others, had each been given a home in the quartier of rue Saint-Jacques, representing—in particular *Val-de-Grâce*—the expression of a petition to the Virgin Mary that Queen Anne would conceive a son.

Mary delivered: the child Louis XIV would lay the first stone of *Val-de-Grâce* when he was seven years old.

His mother's Benedictine convent and the grounds of *Val-de-Grâce,* in the following centuries, became an army hospital, a military school, and a museum, perhaps in memory of Anne's son (Louis XIV loved nothing more than his wars and his victories, celebrated by dances and balls and singing), ignoring how much it all cost.

Inside the high ornate front railings and gates of *Val-de-Grâce* you cross the *cour d'honneur,* a spacious cobblestone courtyard fronting the church with its magnificent façade and Corinthian portico; above it rises the drum with a dome and lantern. Pediments, the symmetrical triangular forms at the top of the classical window and the door beneath it, suggest the authority of the church's tradition. For Catholics, the regularity of that tradition is a sign of the one, holy, and apostolic church. The triangle may also symbolize the doctrine of the Holy Trinity.

After you pay the modest entrance fee in the front vestibule, you can explore the hospital/museum/cloisters inside a labyrinth of corridors, sit in the garden bordering the cloisters where Anne once prayed and visited the nuns; nearby is the wide royal stairway to the second floor where you find the chapel.

If you're lucky, you might find a chamber music ensemble or a choir rehearsing on a Saturday afternoon for one of the superb *Val-de-Grâce Sunday concerts*. Mostly, though, it's the Baroque splendor of architecture and decoration that takes you away from the moment you cross the chapel's threshold: the high altar, its six huge swirling twisting columns, a surround of gold and colored marble, modeled on Bernini's baldachin in Saint Peter's in Rome. The sculpted Nativity, the original now in Saint-Roch; in a side chapel, a painting of the devout foundress/determined mother, Anne of Austria, surrounded by angels. The choir is to the right of the high altar. Except for rehearsing musicians, *Val-de-Grâce* is usually empty, not a sound except, perhaps, for the whispers of a few visitors. There's also the extreme opulence of its ambiance, gold and marble, marble and gold, on the ceiling, the walls, the altar, the floor, the statues. The taste of the Bourbon kings and queens and their artisans had changed since early Christianity's tradition of "solidarity with the needs of the poor."

There is a secretive feeling here, along the empty corridors of the former monastery. That might be because historically the military hospital, off in the wings and behind the closed doors, has only admitted military heroes and men of power in need of medical care. The dignitaries arrive in secret, via unmarked helicopters landing inside the hospital's rear gates on boulevard de Port-Royal.

It was no secret, however, when *Abbé Pierre* (1912–2007), the most renowned religious/military hero of twentieth-century France, was admitted to this hospital in January 2007. And within a few days, thousands of Parisians were waiting in long lines in the freezing cold courtyard and along *rue Saint-Jacques* to attend Abbé Pierre's wake in the *Val-de-Grâce chapel*. On January 26, when the hearse left the *cour d'honneur* to take Abbé Pierre's body down the hill to his funeral at *Notre-Dame,* the mourners followed. They included the president of France, parliamentarians, union members, refugees, the homeless and ordinary citizens, priests, nuns, bishops, workers, illegal aliens. The front seats in the cathedral, usually reserved for dignitaries, were occupied, according to *Abbé Pierre*'s last wishes, by his friends: the homeless, the ragpickers, scavengers, ex-cons, bums, his coworkers at *Emmaus House,* the organization he'd begun and managed after the brutal winter of 1954 when the homeless and the evicted of Paris were starving and freezing to death on the wide boulevards, under the bridges. Caring for the rejected poor had been Abbé Pierre's life's work. An authentic Christian, he was voted the most popular man in France for almost forty years, until 2003 when the great soccer champion Zinedine Zidane took the title. (*Abbé Pierre* had tried to have his name removed from the annual popularity poll.)

His name at birth was Henri Marie Joseph Grouès. In France he was known as *Abbé Pierre*. (*Abbé* means "abbot" in French, a courtesy title given to Catholic priests in French-speaking countries; the root is *abba*, "father.") But he was a nobody, having no power of the kind respected by the ecclesiastical hierarchy or the high priests of finance or politics. He and his companions had at times to beg for their supper. As a boy, his hero was *Francis of Assisi*; Assisi itself enchanted him, the greenness of the mountain valleys, the sheltering mountainsides of Umbria. The saint and the Umbrian mountains stayed with Grouès. He was ordained a priest in 1938. It was an irony of ironies, maybe an absurdity, that at the end, *Abbé Pierre*, the tall thin man with the naked feet inside broken sandals and the worn black cassock, was mourned by the powerful in such magisterial settings as the *church of Val-de-Grâce* and the *Cathedral of Notre-Dame*.

He had a brilliant military record, having served as a Resistance leader of the *maquis* in the Vercors Plateau and the Chartreuse Mountains, which saw some of World War II's fiercest anti-Nazi combat. He helped hunted Jews and *résistants* escape over the Alps to Switzerland. Arrested, wounded, he escaped Nazi prisons many times, to Spain, to North Africa. His years in the Resistance, he said later, taught him the absolute obligation to engage in civil disobedience in the face of assaults on human rights.

After the war, he worked at *Combat* in Paris with Albert Camus and entered politics in the National Assembly as an elected deputy for poor districts. Paris was crowded with the homeless and starving refugees after the war. They huddled under the quay bridges along the waterfronts; they lived out of sight in the shacks and squats in the new suburbs.

Quitting politics, Abbé Pierre invested his deputy's salary in a dump of a house in Neuilly in western Paris. With his derelict friends he restored the place, naming it "Emmaus" after a village in Israel where, in the gospel of Luke, two strangers offered hospitality to Jesus just after his resurrection, without recognizing him. (Rembrandt's painting, *Christ at Emmaus,* hangs in the Louvre; and others in the Mansart Chapel of *Saint-Séverin* [p. 33] and *Saint-Merri* [p. 149].)

This first reconstruction of a derelict building for the use of the homeless marked the beginning of the worldwide *Emmaus* movement, supported by donations and the sale of clothing that volunteers to this day make and refurbish themselves. (*Emmaus* retail shops are everywhere in Paris; most display a poster of *Abbé Pierre* in the front window.)

During the catastrophe of the winter of 1953–1954, *Abbé Pierre* became famous. For months, the temperatures had fallen below fifteen degrees, the waters of the Canal Saint-Martin and the Seine froze, food supplies were stuck in the ice, the homeless poor in the streets.

On February 1, 1954, *Abbé Pierre* gave a speech on Radio Luxembourg that *Le Figaro* printed:

My friends, come help. . . . A woman froze to death tonight at 3 A.M. on the pavement of boulevard de Sébastopol, clutching the eviction notice which the day before had made her homeless. . . . Each night, more than two thousand endure the cold, without food, without bread, more than one almost naked. . . . Hear me: in the last three hours, two aid centers have been created: one under canvas at the foot of the Panthéon, on rue de la Montagne Sainte-Geneviève, the other in Courbevoie. They are already overflowing, we must open them everywhere. I beg of you, let us love one another enough to do it now. From so much pain, let a wonderful thing be given unto us: the shared spirit of France. . . . We need tonight, five thousand blankets, three hundred big American tents, and two hundred stoves. Bring them quickly . . . tonight at eleven, in front of the tent on Montagne Sainte-Geneviève. Thanks to you, no man, no child will sleep on the asphalt or on the waterfronts of Paris tonight.

Supplies poured in, along with volunteers and donations exceeding five hundred million francs (Charlie Chaplin gave two million). The press named that night *l'insurrection de la bonté*, the uprising of kindness. At Abbé Pierre's urging, Paris opened the métro stations at night as places of shelter until the frigid weather passed.

Forever after February 1, 1954, France loved Abbé Pierre. He had awakened her soul. He was their number one citizen until he died in 2007.

His *Emmaus House* mission took him to many countries, seeking donations, making friends among Muslims, Jews, Buddhists, Orthodox Christians. Not constrained by his movement's need for donations, he criticized the apartheid regime in South Africa, the IMF for its oppression of the Third World, the violence in Sarajevo, the Gulf War of George H. W. Bush and Saddam Hussein, the abuse of Palestinians. The poor, he said, are the victims of war. Always. He criticized the Vatican for its lavish lifestyle, the limousines, palaces, the miters, the expensive jet-setting of John Paul II. (On the day he was ordained, the Jesuit and author Henri de

Lubac told him: Ask the Holy Spirit to grant you the same anticlericalism of the saints.)

Abbé Pierre acknowledged having had a sexual relationship in the thirties and later a platonic passion for a woman in a choir who had "a voice like an angel." He supported a married clergy, women priests, contraception when the AIDS epidemic struck; he did not condemn homosexuality. He did not condemn the liberation theology of Latin American priests; in his lifetime it was condemned by the Vatican, the U.S. government, and Christopher Hitchens in his book *God Is Not Great*. In rebuttal, the Irish writer/philosopher Terry Eagleton wrote:

> *All authentic theology is liberation theology. All religions are authentic that practice love and mercy toward the destitute and dispossessed. The* anawim *is Saint Paul's word: the shit of the earth, the scum and refuse of society.*

In the end, the splendid chapel of *Val-de-Grâce* was an appropriate setting for *Abbé Pierre*'s wake. His mission was as extreme in faith as the chapel's extravagant high altar. As a veteran of World War II and a Resistance hero, he spent his last days in *Val-de-Grâce*'s military hospital, dying from a chronic lung disease. The pope, Benedict XVI, ignored his death at first, later sending a scroll. On a plaque outside *Emmaus* headquarters in *Romainville,* Belleville (surrounded by the streets where Édith Piaf learned to sing as a child and survive as a single mother), *Abbé Pierre* inscribed what he wanted in the way of honors when he died:

> *On my grave no flowers or wreath. But a list of the families that you provided with keys to a decent house. . . . The language of love is what you do.*

Nearby

SCHOLA CANTORUM: *A short walk north of Val-de-Grâce at no. 269, rue Saint-Jacques, one of the oldest private schools of music in Paris. A beautiful interior with concerts to match. For tickets, www.classictic.com/en/Paris.*

Related Readings

Terry Eagleton, *Reason, Faith, and Revolution: Reflections on the God Debate*

Denis R. McNamara, *How to Read Churches: A Course in Ecclesiastical Architecture*

Saint-Médard

SAINT-MÉDARD

LOCATION: 39–41, RUE DAUBENTON, AT THE FOOT OF RUE
   MOUFFETARD
HOURS: Mon, 5–7:30; Tues–Fri, 8–12:30 and 2:30–7:30;
   Sat, 9–12:30, 2:30–7:30; Sun, 8:30–12:30 and 4–8
MÉTRO: le Monge

The Church of Saint-Médard has a history that matches the history of religion in France: it's fierce, militant; it's deranged. The church's mix of Gothic, Flamboyant Gothic, and Renaissance styles contributes to a sense of *Saint-Médard*'s multiple personalities.

The church you find today dates from 1400; there was an earlier one under the protection of the abbey of *Saint-Germain-des-Prés* (see p. 77). In the centuries that followed, as the bitter Reformation, the civil Wars of Religion, and the persecution of heretics gathered force, *Saint-Médard* became a battleground.

Visiting at noontime, I entered through the red front door that faces *rue Mouffetard*. I heard singing in the distance. Walking the length of the nave, I followed the music, noting the fluting on the graceful Doric columns. Crossing the ambulatory, I found noon Mass in progress in a lovely chapel— the Lady Chapel—behind the high altar, attended by people of all ages, their singing lovely. The people know the words of the hymns; they're not reading from hymnals. The five con-celebrating priests, in white chasubles, the chapel decked out in Pentecost red, are singing along with them. They have friendly faces. After Communion, there is more singing, grave, like dark velvet. Then another hymn at the priests' blessing of dismissal. *Amen, Amen, Alleluia!* Again, everyone joins in.

Following the Mass, the five priests process out of the Lady Chapel and into the old Gothic church, stopping to shake hands and chat briefly with the Mass goers who approach them. As I walked forward, instead of exiting, into the Lady Chapel to look closely at two paintings on either side of the altar, each man, as he passes me, says the church is now closed. *"Fermé, madame!"* I continued along a side aisle, wanting to look closely at the subjects in the stained-glass windows. I see Clotilde, the pious wife of Clovis; Jeanne de Valois; and I can't make out the third image. *"Fermé,"* says the man who had been the main celebrant and is now rattling a large set of keys behind me. I stayed, kept looking; he walks away toward the front doors of the church.

The lights are turned off just as I moved in close to study the third image in a side chapel window: Is that *Saint Geneviève*, the patron saint of Paris whose courage is commemorated just up the hill of **rue Mouffetard** on **Montagne Sainte-Geneviève?** (See p. 44.)

Suddenly, as I turn away, the priest with the keys is standing in front of me. His friendly face is now not friendly: *"L'église est fermé, Madame! Fermé."* The face that had been so unguarded, almost sweet when he was presiding at the noon Mass in the Lady Chapel: *"Fermé!"*

I followed him at once. He had locked all the front doors and now had to unlock them. Would he have locked me in? I asked him politely why the hurry. I confessed: *"Je suis une touriste."* (I had walked a good distance from the métro, looking for Place du Père Teilhard de Chardin, which turned out to be an uphill nondescript *passage* along winding streets into *rue Mouffetard*. A long detour.)

I wanted to say to the priest that the church is lovely and ask the name of the artist who painted the two wonderful paintings in the rear chapel and another in the chapel of the baptismal font. But he wasn't up for conversation. I didn't dare take another second of his time. He motioned me out through the red front door that he had finally unlocked with a great scowl and a shake of his abundant keys. I understood some of what he said to me, with heavy wheezing, breathing. *"Vite, madame, pour manger, c'est l'heure du déjeuner. L'église est fermé, vous devez . . ."*

Outside, I sat in the pretty square, and wished it were later than 12:30. In the after-school hours, I have seen small children and their caregivers come into the church's gardens and playground that curve along the south side of the church. Their antics, the staccato of their high spirits—the show is always fun, like the dancing and singing that takes place in this square—*La Mouffe*—on Sunday mornings. The street itself has been cleaned up since its origin in 1254. The word *moffettes*, or *mouffettes*, comes from an extremely disagreeable odor along this road to Italy, where tanners worked and polluted the nearby river *Bièvre* with their garbage and stench. *Quelle mouffette!* said the Parisians, trying not to inhale.

Saint-Médard's public gardens, newly landscaped, have been planted on ground that hundreds of years before had held the church's two cemeteries (or maybe one double cemetery). It played a central role in the ongoing Wars of Religion that, for centuries, scarred the souls of Catholics and Protestants in France and beyond. Luther and Calvin's legacy in fiercely Catholic Paris consisted of burned-out churches, censured writers and publishers, and narrow cobblestone streets running with the blood of both Catholic and Protestant mutilated corpses. In 1561, before the Saint Bartholomew's Day Massacre of Protestants in 1572 (see *The Streets of Paris*, pp. 39–41), the Huguenots (Protestants) had attacked the churchgoers at *Saint-Médard* and looted the church. The event is remembered as "*la Tumulte*" in history books. The church remained standing in the fierce fighting that followed the Saint Bartholomew's Day Massacre ten years later. Protestants who hadn't been drowned in the Seine tended to flee to Geneva, La Rochelle, and what became Germany.

The nastiest—and weirdest—part of *Saint-Médard*'s history derives from the theological writings of the bishop of Flanders (in the Netherlands) Cornelius Jansen (1585–1638). His treatise advocated the Protestant/Calvinist belief in predestination and attacked the Jesuits' belief in free will. Jansen's "*Jansenism*" found its way to Paris, where Catholicism was said to have been sugarcoated by the worldly and influential *Jesuits* (they founded and controlled many schools). The Jansenists claimed that Jesuits made it easy for people in feather beds to get to heaven. The fathers were indeed at home in "the world," its theater, opera, singing, and dancing. (Louis XIV, who loved to dance, was fond of the Jesuits until he wasn't.) It was the Sun King who ordered the persecution of the Jansenists and influenced the pope to condemn all Jansenist beliefs and institutions. (The word *Beelzebub* translated at the time as "prince of the Huguenots.") The Jansenist convents of Port-Royal were closed by the king; the nuns, one of whom was the sister of philosopher Blaise Pascal, were arrested. One building in Paris survived as a hospital, still open today, just a few minutes away off boulevard de Port-

Royal. Jansenism exported itself to Ireland, in particular; James Joyce invokes its joyless memory in his autobiographical novel *A Portrait of the Artist as a Young Man*. "*They sleep in their coffins*," the schoolboys said of the French priests.

Some parishioners of *Saint-Médard* developed a taste for Jansenist asceticism. A cleric of the parish, François Pâris, encouraged the Jansenist practices of sleeping on hard wooden boards, wearing hair shirts with spiked belts, lashing themselves with spiked chains before bedtime. Sin was everywhere. God was a meanie. When François Pâris died at the age of thirty-seven, exhausted from his life of self-punishment and abstinence, his disciples lost their minds. At night they gathered around his black marble gravestone in *Saint-Médard*'s cemetery (now the garden) to smash their heads against his tombstone, frothing at the mouth, speaking in tongues, shaking as if epileptic, having convulsions: in short, going hysterical. They, who were mostly women, became known as *les convulsionnaires*. They fastened their dresses at the ankles to keep them from rising above their heads as they contorted like crazed gymnasts. They rolled and jumped and screamed, some seeming to eat their own feces with pleasure. Whether this is fact or fantasy or both, it plays out the theory of the multiple personalities of *Saint-Médard*'s ancestry. François Pâris's grave was said to be the site of miraculous cures; the **convulsionnaires** ate the dirt around it while they cried out, begging to be beaten and tortured. Pain, it seemed, was voluptuous.

The cemetery was closed in 1732 by order of the church and the state. A mysterious anonymous message attached to the gate became part of the church's lore: *De par le Roi, défense à Dieu de faire miracle en ce lieu*. "By order of the King, God is forbidden to perform miracles in this place."

Today's gardens, the setting for the possessed piety of the eighteenth-century *convulsionnaires,* have transformed the *quartier.* They're now given over to the pleasure of children. ***Regarde, maman!*** *La petite* is climbing a tall tree, leafy lush with wide branches and leaves, slanting sun and shade covering the ground. Kids are shrieking, running, parents smile or ignore them.

Nearby

LE BISTRO: *"Les Délices d'Aphrodite"—At rue de Candolle, to the east of* **Saint-Médard,** *paralleling* **rue Mouffetard.** *Perfect.*

GÉRARD PATOUT FLEURISTE: *A beautiful flower shop on the northeast corner of rue Candolle. A movie set? Or just a place to smell the flowers. Some Parisians buy flowers for their homes once a week.*

Related Readings

Jean Lacouture, *Jesuits: A Multibiography*

George Orwell, ***Down and Out in Paris and London***

Grand Mosque of Paris

GRAND MOSQUE OF PARIS

LOCATION: 2, PLACE DU PUITS DE L'ERMITE
HOURS: Sat–Thurs, 9–12 and 2–6
MÉTRO: Censier-Daubenton
WWW.MOSQUEEDEPARIS.NET
DIRECTIONS: Walk east from rue Mouffetard on rue
Daubenton for about five minutes—Saint-Médard and
rue Mouffetard are at your back—and, as the minaret
and green-tiled mosque come into view, turn left and
walk up the hill to 2, Place du Puits de l'Ermite.

The domes of the *Grande Mosquée* of Paris and the golden
mosaics of the minaret pierce the skyline of this eastern
edge of the *Latin Quarter.* The voice of the muezzin from the
top of the minaret calling Muslims to prayer five times a day
adds a background of ancient chant to the sacred site.

Once inside the mosque (admission 3 euros), you enter
the courtyard, a calm bright space of grassy green plantings, turquoise pools of water, lovely tiled walls of white and
black and shades of blue. "The desert culture of Islam," in
the words of Garry Wills, "sees heaven as a garden perpetually rinsed with purifying waters." Palm trees and cypress
rise along the aisles of intricately carved arches and columns
bordering cascading fountains. Rosebushes flower profusely
in June and into high summer.

Walking here, even on gray winter days, you notice the
light from above, brightening the tiled walls, the sounds of
murmuring voices and flowing water stirring a feeling of

reverence. Approaching this place from the plain, nondescript street outside, you'd never dream such a hushed and beautiful sanctuary existed so close by.

Beyond the courtyard is a large dimly lit prayer room for men and women, the floor and walls covered with magnificent carpets. You're free to wander. Other rooms for prayer and study open onto more dim corridors. The prostrated worshippers pray to *Allah,* their god who is a merciful, compassionate god to the pious, though terrible to the unfaithful.

From the *Koran, the Holy Book of Islam*:

> *The God of mercy hath taught the Koran / Hath created man, / Hath taught him articulate speech, / The sun and the moon have each their times, / And the plants and the trees bend in adoration. / And the heaven he hath reared it on high; and he hath appointed the balance, / That in the balance ye should not transgress. . . . And the earth he hath prepared it for the living tribes. . . .*

Religious scholars, in particular Ninian Smart, who quotes many passages from the *Koran* in his book *The Religious Experience,* have noted analogies between the vision of the Hebrew Bible and the *Koran.* Hebrew prophets and holy Muslims are said to experience mystical visions and ecstasies during prayer. There is a similar ethical impulse in both religions, an insistence on righteousness and a condemnation of cheating and idolatry. The first and greatest of Muslim prophets, *Muhammad* (570–632), was influenced by Judaism and Christianity, but the religion he preached was original, having profound effects on history and culture from the seventh century onward.

The downstairs of the mosque, where women perform

their ablutions, is interesting to explore. If you take a guided tour, you can ask about the religious significance of the ritual baths. (Each of the Abrahamic religions—Judaism, Islam, and Christianity—have, in different periods of their history, required special cleansing rites for women, as well as head coverings, though since Vatican II in the sixties, Christian churches have revoked that requirement.)

Besides being a place of prayer, like the Jewish synagogue and the Christian church, the mosque has multiple functions: it has in the past provided apartments to the people who work there, a health and social services clinic, archives, small gardens, a library of ancient manuscripts, steam baths, pools, a restaurant and café. You're free to explore wherever you like, at your leisure.

What many visitors, Parisians and tourists, have never heard of is the hidden history of the *Paris Mosque*: it played an important role in the French Resistance in World War II, until recently a well-kept secret, a neglected story. Just as many people in Arab countries deny the very fact of the Holocaust, so Western historians have failed to note the contribution of the *Grand Mosque* to the rescue of Jews during the Nazi Occupation. Arab Holocaust deniers, however, deny their own history when they ignore this story of courage.

Walking along the corridors, in and out of prayer rooms and a large library, it's easy to imagine the history of this place as a sanctuary of secrets. (See *The Streets of Paris*, pp. 105–12).

It is inarguable that the Occupation years created and sustained a time of interreligious brotherhood between many North African Muslims and many of the hunted Jews of

Paris. Without the mosque, the number of Jewish deaths and deportations would undoubtedly have been higher. In July 1942 when the Nazis and the French police arrested thirteen thousand Jews in the *Vél d'Hiv* roundup, eight thousand of the arrested Jews came from the immigrant neighborhood of *Belleville* in northeastern Paris where many Muslims, worshippers at the *Grand Mosque,* lived. Without the help of the Kabyle spy networks and the availability of the *mosque* as a hiding place, there would have been many more Belleville Jews lost that day.

Wise people saw then and acknowledge now the spiritual bond that has always united the two cultures. "Whoever saves one life," says the Talmud, "it is as if they have saved the whole world." "Whoever saves one life saves the entire world," says the *Koran*. And, as Eric Hazan observes in *The Invention of Paris: A History in Footsteps,* in today's *Belleville* and *Ménilmontant* there is still a multicultural peace: Orthodox Jewish men, mothers in African robes, Chinese and Muslim families shop together in the markets along the *boulevard de Belleville*. I observed Jewish and Muslim children playing together on weekend afternoons in Belleville playgrounds, their convivial parents looking on.

The current state of fundamentalist Islam in the Middle East is a salient reminder that all three religions of the Book—Judaism, Christianity, and Islam—have, throughout history, had their periods of brutality against other religions and peoples. Islam is no more ISIS than Christianity still represents the Inquisition, the torture and murder of heretics.

The *Grand Mosque of Paris* was built between 1922 and 1926 to symbolize the eternal friendship between France and Islam. It was also meant as a sign of gratitude to the half-million Muslims of the French Empire's North African colonies who had fought against the Germans in World War I. A hundred thousand Muslims died for France; without their sacrifice, it is said, the victory of Verdun would not have happened. The *mosque* was particularly meant to honor the fallen Muslim *tirailleurs* (sharpshooters) from Algeria.

The first prayer offered at the **Paris Mosque** in 1926, in the presence of the president of France, was given by the rector who was also the mosque's founder. **Benghabrit**, born in Algeria in 1868, was a cultured diplomat in Paris and North Africa who wrote books, enjoyed Parisian salon culture, and loved music, becoming the most important Muslim in Paris and the most influential Arab in Europe. He has now become an acclaimed figure of historical interest because of his actions during the Holocaust.

When the Nazis and the Vichy government began arresting and deporting the Jews of Paris, **Benghabrit** committed himself and his congregation to making the **Grand Mosque** a sanctuary for endangered Jews. He devised a threefold rescue operation: first, he offered European and Algerian Jews shelter in the same apartments inhabited by Muslim families; second, he gave them fake identity certificates, to prove they were Muslims, not Jews; finally, he initiated the use of the cellars and tunnels beneath the mosque as escape routes. The Jews in hiding crawled and dug their way through the sewers and tunnels (*souterrains)* under the *mosque* to the banks of the Seine where empty wine barges and boats operated by Kabyles were waiting to smuggle them out of Occupied Paris.

There are many more stories and characters who appear in the history of the Muslims' protection and rescue of Jews. Benghabrit risked his life each time the Gestapo barged in and searched the premises. (See *The Grand Mosque of Paris:*

A Story of How Muslims Rescued Jews During the Holocaust by Karen Gray Ruelle and Deborah Durland DeSaix.)

Not much data is available to provide the exact numbers of Jews rescued by the *mosque*. But what does exist— newspapers, scholarly research (Robert Satloff, *Among the Righteous: Lost Stories of the Holocaust's Long Reach into Arab Lands*), and personal testimonies from Jews who, after the war, told of hiding in the mosque's basements—supports the details of this hidden history.

Benghabrit was given the *Grand Croix de Légion d'Honneur* after the war. But Eva Wiesel has noted in the *New York Times* that getting Yad Vashem in Israel to grant the honorific of "Righteous Among Nations" to a Muslim, even the Oscar Schindler–like Benghabrit, is and will remain very difficult. This unsung leader of the *Paris Mosque Resistance* died in 1954 in the early stages of the war of Algerian independence. He is buried in the *mosque*, facing east in the direction of Mecca, as are all Muslims.

Nearby

MOSQUE GARDEN AND TEAROOM: *Open daily, 9 A.M.– midnight. Around the block from the mosque entrance, on the corner of **Daubenton and 39, rue Geoffroy Sainte-Hilaire**, opposite the **Jardin des Plantes**. A pretty terrace café, with jasmine, and olive and fig trees, and many singing birds in a surround of dark blue and turquoise mosaics. Weekdays peaceful, weekends crowded and loud.*

JARDIN DES PLANTES: *Walk directly across the street from the mosque tearoom to enter the **Jardin des Plantes**. Continue walking east through the garden (toward the **Seine**)—along a* *gorgeous promenade between flower beds—(detour left to the Al-pine Gardens). Stop at the **National Museum of Natural History** at the corner entrance at 2, rue Buffon. The paleontologist/theologian **Pierre Teilhard de Chardin (1881–1955)** worked here in the Galleries of Paleontology, a long iron-framed building with a glass ceiling and fine balustrades (and many skeletons of reptiles, mammals, dinosaurs, and mammoths). A metal ramp takes you up to the top level, full of amazing fossilized skeletons, where Teilhard's labs were.*

*After World War I, Teilhard looked back on his years here with joy, walking in the gardens with colleagues, discussing science and religion in the labs. There was no difference, he said, between research and the adoration of God. A few of his writings can be found in the museum's **gift shop** on the ground floor.*

*A popular professor and researcher, Teilhard was dismissed from his work in paleontology and his teaching post at the **Institut Catholique** in **rue d'Assas** (see p. 98), where he was Chair of Geology: his Jesuit superior thought a lecture he gave at the Sorbonne sounded like Darwinist heresy, an attack on Catholic doctrine, specifically the "Garden of Eden" story (or the "Genesis fable"). He alerted Rome, and Teilhard became a Jesuit with a "record." An evolutionist, he was way ahead of his time in the Church. He was exiled to China (seven times until his death) and forbidden to publish or lecture in Paris.*

Teilhard saw no contradiction between science and religion, between Christianity and evolution, the notion of a Cosmos "in the process of limitless, endless change," to quote biographer Jean Lacouture. In China, Paris, and New York (another place of exile), Teilhard continued writing his masterworks, The Phenomenon of Man, *published posthumously in 1955, an instant international success, and* The Divine Milieu *(1957), a beautiful work, still in print and selling well.*

Thousands of papers, books, and conferences have now been devoted to the mysticism of his theology and philosophy. "How can we not compare the two great figures of Teilhard and Galileo?" asked one Jesuit scholar. He had, in his own words, "the dream of every mystic, the eternal pantheist dream." The deeper he went into science, the surer he felt there was a God. God is all in all. (Or in the words of van Gogh, "God is in everything, except the church and my bloody family.")

There is a large bronze plaque about Teilhard across from the Jardin des Plantes in the Square of the Arsenal on Quai Henri IV.

INSTITUTE DU MONDE ARABE: *1, rue des Fossés-Saint-Bernard, entrance through the south-side façade; daily except Mon, 10–6. A glass gem of a building by Jean Nouvel, one of France's great architects, overlooking the Seine from the Left Bank. From the ninth-floor terrace the views (and the Lebanese food) are wonderful. The gift shop on the main floor offers an excellent selection of fine fabrics and pottery in exquisite Islamic designs and colors. Return toward the* **mosque,** *passing the* **Grande Galerie de l'Évolution** *near the entrance to* **Jardin des Plantes.** *(Open Weds–Mon, 10–6; closed Tues, May 1. Exciting exhibits, on three levels. Long lines for admission.)*

Related Readings

Margaret Smith, *Muslim Women Mystics: The Life and Work of Rábi'a and Other Women Mystics in Islam*

Farid al-Din Attar, *Muslim Saints and Mystics*

Pierre Teilhard de Chardin, *The Divine Milieu*

Anthony Doerr, *All the Light We Cannot See*

Garry Wills, *What the Qu'Ran Meant and Why It Matters*

Saint-Germain-des-Prés

Saint-Germain

SAINT-GERMAIN-DES-PRÉS

LOCATION: I, PLACE SAINT-GERMAIN-DES-PRÉS
HOURS: 8—7
MÉTRO: Saint-Germain
WWW.EGLISE-SGP.ORG

It's hard to know where to begin. First, perhaps, by begging the traveler/reader's pardon: for exaggeration, hyperbole, call it what you will. Because for me, *Saint-Germain-des-Prés* is the loveliest church in Paris. I've been visiting her since my first long-ago trip to Paris. I learned about *Saint-Germain* in a college art history course. The professor told the truth about its beauty. So did her slides. So, I hope, did King Chilperic about the abbot, *Germain des Prés*: Germain of the Fields. *"He was a father, and a shepherd to his people, who loved him."*

In the beginning the church was part of the Benedictine abbey founded here by Childebert (reigned 511–558), son of King Clovis (see p. 79). Here Childebert housed the relics he brought back from a crusade to Spain. Although parts of the *Church of Saint-Germain-des-Prés* have been rebuilt and restored many times, it remains the oldest church in Paris and one of the few that still shows some of its Romanesque origins.

The bell tower—*la tour-clocher*—of *Saint-Germain-des-Prés* rises from the northwest corner of the *Place* to dominate and charm the streets below. Square, simple, without ornament, it has become the symbol of this part of the city. The *Blue Guide* calls it "reassuring" and "revered." Without question it enjoys the pride of the *Place* that was created in 1866 on the site of the ancient church square. The prospect delights guests of the *Café des Deux Magots* just across the way where you can enjoy *"Instants d'éternité et de légèreté"* ("moments of eternity and lightness")—seated on its corner terrace at midnight, drinking, savoring the company of friends; it delights the *flaneur* who from morning till long after dark feels steeped in history on this corner of Paris.

Studying the *Place,* history aficionados (or religious fanatics) may recall an episode from the long-ago sixteenth-century Wars of Religion when two Huguenots, in 1557, were caught at a secret Protestant service and told to renounce their heresy: abjuring would buy them some leniency. The rest of the story is so gory, I leave it up to the reader to decide whether to make it part of your lore about *Saint-Germain*. (Check out "Walk No. 3, Saint-Germain-des-Prés," in *Pariswalks* by Alison and Sonia Landes.)

During the September Massacres of 1792 and the Terror of 1793–1794, hundreds of monks attached to the *Saint-Germain abbey* had their heads severed on the *Place* and in *Saint-Germain*'s gardens, like their confreres south of the boulevard in the garden and courtyard of *Saint-Joseph-des-Carmes* (see p. 93). In the end, thousands died, here, on the Left Bank, and over the hills of Montmartre in *Saint-Denis* (see p. 187).

Before Paris became Paris, in Roman and Merovingian times, when the *Place* had been a stretch of open fields (*prés*), a temple to the Egyptian goddess Isis had stood on the site where the church now stands. (Isis, goddess of magic, fertility, motherhood, death, healing, and rebirth, was the sister and wife of Osiris, god of the underworld. Her cult spread throughout the Roman Empire where she was worshipped from England to Afghanistan and is now revered by the Wiccan religion.)

By the late fifth to sixth centuries, the cult of Isis had lost its magic, at least in Paris. Her temple disappeared.

Clovis and son Childebert were Christian rulers; and it is believed that in the early sixth century Childebert undertook the building of the beautiful *Chapelle Saint-Symphorien* just at the entrance to *Saint-Germain*. *Saint-Germain* (496–576) was Bishop of Paris. *Symphorien* was from Autun (in Burgundy), and the first Christian martyr in Gaul—his crime was to have ridiculed a pagan image. The entrance to the *chapelle* is to your right—on the church's south side—just before you enter the main church. The *chapelle* was in ancient times the *Merovingian* necropolis (descendants of the pagan *Merovee*, or *Merowech*), who wore their hair down to their waist or their feet, and were buried here, as was Childebert.

The simple interior of the chapel is lit by windows like skylights high in the bright white walls. Here and there you can see fragments of eleventh-century frescoes. *Chapelle Saint-Symphorien,* radiant with light, was restored to its original design between 1970 and 1992. Today noon Masses, well attended by Parisians, are celebrated here, as are baptisms.

On the Right and Left Banks of the Seine, there were small hillocks (*monceaux*), leftovers from the pagan temples over which many churches were built once the pagans had moved on. There's not a trace of Isis's temple. The pagan temples at *Montmartre* were replaced by a church on the site of Saint Denis's martyrdom: the *mons Mercure*, "Mercury's mount." The ancient temple to *Bacchus* on top of what would come to be called *Montagne Sainte-Geneviève* was replaced by the Place du Panthéon. A temple to Jupiter, and below that a druid altar, were found in the depths of *Notre-Dame* (p. 11).

Temples come and temples go, leaving behind not only stone fragments but bizarre stories from ancient history. Sometimes it's a jolt to keep in mind: *we are made of history.*

By the twentieth century, after much damage to *Saint-Germain-des-Prés*'s interior inflicted over the centuries by ninth-century Vikings (or Norsemen), warring Catholics and Protestants in the fifteenth through seventeenth centuries, the 1789 Revolution, the June Days of 1848, the Commune of 1871—each a campaign of barbaric pillage, anticlericalism, anti-monarchism, and the random slaughter of sansculottes and radicals—a total restoration and cleaning of the church's interior was initiated. It just recently, in 2020, came to a glorious conclusion.

There is so much beauty inside *Saint-Germain-des-Prés*. To make sure you don't miss any of the details, I recommend you stop in the bookshop directly across from *Chapelle Saint-Symphorien* and pick up the excellent guide/booklet "Saint-Germain-des-Prés Down the Ages" (10 euros). The maps, photos, text, captions are excellent. The exquisite photograph of the statue *The Virgin of the Smile* (1250), on p. 37, a new addition to the church, was only recently discovered in a dig in Place de Furstemberg (1999). The more sober statue, *Our Lady of Consolation* (1340), was discovered in the fourteenth century. (See p. 51.) The restored sanctuary—the original floor, the Crossing of the transept, the entire furniture of the liturgical set, composed of marble from the Pyrenees, the new choir stalls, the tabernacle, and the cross of Glory—the new sanctuary projects a perfect harmony.

Many elements created or rediscovered in the course of many restorations are intact (though recently repainted in magnificent blue, red, green, gold. The website offers a good sample of images.). The newly restored nave (first completed around 1050), seventy-one yards long, is a mixture of styles: the main body is Romanesque; the chancel is Gothic; the choir with its ribbed vaults and the ambulatory with the nine lovely radiating chapels are twelfth century. Of the capitals in the middle aisle, twenty-two are original.

But it's *La Vierge du Sourire* (the Virgin of the Smile), her head tilted toward the baby, the feeling of tenderness and pleasure between mother and child that makes the church a place you'll never forget and will always want to visit on your walks along the Left Bank. You have to look for *La Vierge,* no matter what the booklet tells you. I've found her next to the main altar and a few months later in one of the apse chapels. Art historians have called her "the Mona Lisa of the Middle Ages." She is a contemporary of the Smiling Angel of Reims, another jewel of the thirteenth century. *L'Ange du Sourire* is on the western façade of Reims Cathedral where Clovis was crowned king in the fifth century, Reims (or Rheims in the UK) becoming the traditional setting for the coronation of the kings of France.

Pope Alexander III consecrated *Saint-Germain-des-Prés* a few weeks before he laid the first stone of the *Cathedral of Notre-Dame* in 1163.

For all the magnificence of the new *Saint-Germain-des-Prés,* there is no denying the point of view of literary critic Terry Eagleton in his book *Reason, Faith, and Revolution: Reflections on the God Debate:*

> *Religion has wrought untold misery in human affairs. For the most part, it has been a squalid tale of bigotry, superstition, wishful thinking, and oppressive ideology.*

Yet the ancient people who built and rebuilt their church here, century upon century, were not blinded by its history. They knew the cruelty of their tradition.

They could at the same time imagine the light of the beatitudes. The mysterious peace of the light falling through the stained glass windows. Of the Virgin's Smile. Their imagination lives on: you can hear it in the many concerts performed at night in the nave of *Saint-Germain-des-Prés*. It lives in the singing of choirs, the harmonies of the orchestra, and in the seriousness and smiles of the people.

For schedules and programs, see the website and the posters hung at the top of the métro exit and at the door of the church. Mozart, Bach, Gospel, performed by orchestras, choirs, and the children's choirs of local churches. Summer, fall, winter, and spring. 8:30, tickets online or at the door.

Nearby (see The Streets of Paris, pp. 134–36)

BRASSERIE LIPP: *151, boulevard Saint-Germain. Tel: 01 45 48 53 91. Reserve. Mirrors, mosaics, ceramic designs. Excellent Alsatian food.*

CAFÉ DE FLORE: *172, boulevard Saint-Germain at Place Saint-Germain or Place Jean-Paul-Sartre—Simone-de-Beauvoir). Legendary.*

LE PETIT SAINT BENOÎT: *4, rue Saint-Benoît near the corner of rue Jacob. A wonderful 150-year-old bistro. Antoine de Saint-Exupéry's favorite. And Camus's. And Marguerite Duras's.*

MUSÉE NATIONAL EUGÈNE DELACROIX: *6, Place de Furstemberg. Métro: Saint-Germain. Hours: daily except Tues, 9:30–5. Walk straight along rue de l'Abbaye from the bell tower* on *Place Saint-Germain. Turn left, off rue de l'Abbaye, which parallels the church of* **Saint-Germain**. *Enter the lovely square where Delacroix's apartment and studio—now a museum—is on the west side. Behind his apartment is his garden, a delightful sanctuary. If you read his* Journal, *on sale at the gift shop, you'll know how much this garden meant to him. It was like a church sanctuary where he contemplated and imagined. He knew Paris intimately. He found his sources in the Jardins des Plantes; the Luxembourg Gardens; the Louvre; in the studios of his friends, especially his dear friend Frédéric Chopin. Paris, he said, gave him "the beauty of the world."*

COUR DU MÛRIER DES BEAUX ARTS: *14, rue Bonaparte. Just north of the church, toward the Seine, on the west side of the street, between Quai Malaquais and rue Bonaparte. The cloister, situated in the interior of the* **École Nationale des Beaux Arts***, a subsidiary of the* **Institut de France***, is quiet and solitary, so still and thick with chestnut trees. The chapel and the cloister, once part of the convent of Petits Augustins, has arcades, fountains, sculptures. Few visitors. Open irregularly, usually on Monday afternoons and holidays. Rodin was rejected for admission here three times, Matisse four times. Delacroix, Degas, Fragonard, Renoir, and Charles Garnier attended.*

Related Readings

Saint Benedict's Rule for Monasteries

Stacy Schiff, *Saint-Exupéry*

Albert Camus, *Notebooks: 1942–1951; Notebooks: 1951–1959*

Saint-Sulpice

SAINT-SULPICE

LOCATION: **PLACE SAINT-SULPICE, EAST SIDE; 2, RUE PALATINE**

HOURS: 8–7:30; guided visits: Sat, 2:30–5:30 (meet at the sacristy); Sun, 2:30; Sunday Masses: 7, 9, 11, 6:45; weekday Masses: 7, 9, 12:05, 6:45

MÉTRO: Saint-Sulpice

Saint-Sulpice gets mixed reviews because it presents mixed identities, some popular, some brilliant, others creepy and laced with dark shadows. The same critics who dislike *Saint-Étienne-du-Mont* have the same word for *Saint-Sulpice*: it's a hodgepodge. Some recall the historical events that complicate the church's reputation: the baptisms of the Marquis de Sade and poet Charles Baudelaire, the marriage of Victor Hugo, the funerals of Francis Poulenc and Jacques Chirac. Your reaction to *Saint-Sulpice* may depend on the time of day or the season when you visit. Voltaire hated it in all seasons, called it ugly. More than the church, he hated its parish priests who badgered him on his deathbed to confess his sins and escape an eternity of hell. It was the Catholic novelist François Mauriac's favorite parish church. In his *Notebooks* he said it reminded him of the music of Poulenc: *"Everything is composed with great spirituality, but also with a charm, grace, and lightheartedness that is basically a form of modesty."*

The "Cathedral of the Left Bank" is only slightly smaller than the *Cathedral of Notre-Dame*; it attracts far fewer tourists (except now, when *Notre-Dame* is closed for reconstruction).

When Dan Brown's novel *The Da Vinci Code* appeared, plotting the presence of a pagan gnomon in the church, an astronomical device linked to a murderous monk plot, all of it was dismissed by the church as hokey fiction: *Contrary to fanciful allegations in a recent best-selling novel,* reads a sign, *this is not a vestige of a pagan temple. No such temple ever existed in this place.* Ron Howard, director of the novel's movie version, was refused permission to film inside the church.

Nowadays *Saint-Sulpice* is cherished in Paris for its superb performances of sacred music (*tickets at FNAC or at the entrance to the church the night of the concert; schedules at www.stsulpice.com*).

On November 9, 2018, the one-hundredth anniversary of the end of World War I—"the Great War" in which France lost eight and a half million men—I sat in the nave in a sold-out performance to hear the *Verdi Requiem* performed by the *Orchestre Hélios* conducted by *Hugues Reiner.* The fifteen hundred concertgoers sat in silence for two hours and then stood in rapturous applause for the gift of this music, a tribute to France's memory of grief.

The church's interior, begun in 1646, finished a century later, was designed by at least six different architects, but the most renowned was the Florentine Giovanni Servandoni, a manager of theater sets, which is obvious when you look at the spread of this very theatrical church. The highlights include the spectacular organ of seven thousand pipes, said to be the largest in Europe. (Lovers of organ music meet after the 11 A.M. Sunday Mass and/or at 2:30 on Sundays at the back of the church under the organ loft to climb the spiral staircase to see the huge instrument over which a portrait of the god of organists, Johann Sebastian Bach, smiles.)

Looking down over the church from the loft, you can study the long nave with its many columns, side aisles, and eight chapels on either side, making the church resemble a Roman basilica. Some of it is painted "gray as old newspaper," to quote Jean-Paul Kauffmann's first-rate book *The Struggle with the Angel: Delacroix, Jacob, and the God of Good and Evil.* The domed Lady Chapel at the east end, behind the apse, is gorgeous on bright days with light falling into the church through the clerestory windows. The marble Virgin behind the altar was carved by Jean-Baptiste Pigalle. (You can see it distinctly from seats in the rear of the nave.) The sacristy on the church's south side is decorated with exquisite carved woodwork. The marble holy water fonts (stoups) on either side of the front door, a gift from Venice to King François I, have the shape of clamshells.

High above the nave, in a kind of second story, are many artists' studios, workshops, storage rooms, hidden out of sight. Beneath the nave, hidden away in the basement, are crypts (one small crypt for an orthodox Copt community of two hundred members) and many storage spaces. It's a labyrinth. You are not free to wander above or below the main church without a guide. On the second and fourth Sundays of each month at three o'clock, the Orthodox Crypt is open to visitors and for concerts.

The most famous place in the church is the ***Chapelle des Saints-Anges*** (the Chapel of the Holy Angels), on the right as you enter the church through a leather-padded front door. The Romantic painter Eugène Delacroix (1798–1863) painted the chapel's three murals from 1849 until he died in 1863; it's no exaggeration to say that the commission killed him. He spent many years preparing the walls and even scaling the east and west sides of the chapel, starting his work with the east panel, *Jacob Wrestling with the Angel* (the story from Genesis 32); and on the west panel with the brutal and shadowy *Heliodorus Driven from the Temple* (from 2 Maccabees 3); on the ceiling of the chapel's dome the subject was *Saint-Michael's Victory over Lucifer*. Delacroix fell off his ladder more than once; he almost gave up the project several times. He told his cousin the work "had become the nightmare of my days." He liked to paint high up on his ladder while the organist was practicing Delacroix's favorite music, the **Dies Irae** from the Mass for the Dead. His own life was full of secrets and sorrow; grief was a theme he knew intimately. It made a certain sense that Delacroix, remembered in art history as a "romantic visionary," had Frédéric Chopin for his favorite friend in Paris. As he grew older, Delacroix felt drawn back to the Catholicism of his childhood, according to Chopin's biographer Benita Eisler; as he listened to Chopin play the piano, he felt "God's presence descending through his fingers."

Only daylight, best in September according to Kauffmann's book, shows the radiance and sparkle of Delacroix's colors. Van Gogh, who considered Delacroix the greatest colorist in the history of French painting, praised his hero's volcanic creativity. He said he painted like a lion devouring its meat (*"comme le lion qui devore le morceau"*). Baudelaire, Delacroix's on-again, off-again friend, saw cruelty in Delacroix's passionate characters and intensely passionate colors; he praised the cruel streak, ignoring the tenderness of Delacroix's art. The east panel, *Jacob Wrestling with the Angel*, according to many interpretations, depicts the confrontation and conflict between God and man, Jacob's soul and body. After the wrestling match, man, though living, is a wounded and eternally conflicted creature. Or, in Kauffmann's words, "we are forever at war with ourselves." We feel but cannot solve the problem of evil.

(There is no such anguish in Rembrandt's *Jacob Wrestling with the Angel* [c. 1659], now in the Gemäldegalerie, Berlin. The two paintings realize two opposite modes of religious experience, one of resistance and fury, one of a contemplative acceptance.)

In winter, make a morning visit to *Saint-Sulpice*; if you wait until afternoon, you'll miss the miracle of light and shadow mixing with Delacroix's colors.

He lived about ten minutes away in his studio and apartment on the charming *Place de Furstemberg* (see p. 82), off the narrow *rue de l'Abbaye* that parallels the church of *Saint-Germain-des-Prés*. In the stillness of his garden, behind the studio (now a museum with gift shop), he found a place to contemplate the beauty of the natural world as well as his visions of color as they might dramatize the contours of reality. "*God is within us,*" he wrote in his *Journal*—("perhaps the greatest literary testament any painter has left," wrote editor Hubert Wellington)—"*God is the inner presence that causes us to admire the beautiful.*"

Outside *Saint-Sulpice,* facing its mismatched towers (*like "two giant clarinets and that is as good a shape as any other,"* said Victor Hugo, one a circle, the other a square)—from the center of *Place Saint-Sulpice,* is the *Fontaine des quatre-évêques* (Fountain of the Four Bishops, 1844). This entire generous space is beloved by Parisians, on lush summer evenings and on frigid February nights. Seasonal markets—a Christmas Fair in December, an Antiques Fair in June—are popular and worth your time, as is the *terrasse* of the *Café de la Mairie* (named for the city hall of the sixth *arrondissement*); the café faces the *Place* from its northeast corner at no. 8, a neighborhood favorite where Albert Camus read his morning newspaper (see *The Streets of Paris*, p. 129) on his way to the office at the publisher Gallimard.

Three lovely sixteenth- and seventeenth-century narrow streets lead south from the *Place Saint-Sulpice* to *rue de Vaugirard* and the *Luxembourg Gardens: rue Garancière* (sixteenth century); the curving *rue Servandoni,* charming twin of the next street, *rue Férou,* where Arthur Rimbaud's poem "Le Bateau ivre" (The Drunken Boat) is inscribed on the wall nearest the *Place.* Chestnut and plane trees and random water fountains make the entire *quartier* delightful to wander under the spell of *Saint-Sulpice.*

Nearby

À LA MÈRE DE FAMILLE: *The oldest and **perhaps** most beloved sweet shop in Paris, opened in 1761, now a chain. 70, rue Bonaparte. Hours: Mon–Sat, 9:30–8.*

HÔTEL LUTETIA: *45, boulevard Raspail, a fifteen-minute walk from **Saint-Sulpice**. One of Paris's loveliest, and, following a recent restoration, most chic hotels, near the Sèvres-Babylone métro. Teatime, happy hour, and dinner, each is a treat you will never forget. Joyce and James, Matisse, Picasso, Sartre, and Camus also liked it. During the Occupation, the Gestapo was installed here; afterward, the Nazis returned the POWs and concentration camp survivors here, as recounted in Marguerite Duras's* The War, *published in French as* La Douleur.

SQUARE BOUCICAUT: *Opposite the **Lutetia,** with entrances at rue de Sèvres, rue de Babylone, rue Velpeau, and boulevard Ra-*

spail. *A lovely square of thick exotic greenery and tall trees, created in memory of Aristide Boucicaut and his wife, Marguerite, the founders of the Bon Marché department store, the oldest in Paris, just across the street. The Boucicauts were two of the most generous philanthropists in the city's history.*

Related Reading

Anne Enright, *The Pleasure of Eliza Lynch*

Jean-Paul Kauffmann, *The Struggle with the Angel: Delacroix, Jacob, and the God of Good and Evil*

Marguerite Duras, *Wartime Notebooks*

Saint-Joseph-des-Carmes

SAINT-JOSEPH-DES-CARMES

LOCATION: 70, RUE DE VAUGIRARD, BETWEEN RUE
   D'ASSAS AND RUE CASSETTE
HOURS: Mass weekdays, Sept–July, 12:15; Sat Mass, 6;
   guided tours of church and crypt, Sat, 3. Access to
   church *70, rue de Vaugirard*
MÉTRO: Rennes; Saint-Placide
WWW.SJDC.FR

The first time I crossed the cobblestone courtyard leading to the domed church of *Saint Joseph-des-Carmes*—a five-minute walk southwest of *Saint-Sulpice*—I stooped to look closely at the ancient stones. I'd heard that you could still see bloodstains on them; no amount of scrubbing had made them disappear in the almost two-and-a-half centuries since the September Massacres of 1792. The new revolutionary National Guard troops as well as the sansculottes had invaded the Carmelite quarters—the monks' cells, called the *Carmes*—late in the afternoon of September 2 and dragged one hundred and twenty priests into the church courtyard. *Les septembriseurs.* Armed with axes, spikes, swords, and pistols, they massacred them. *"Vive la Nation!"* *"Mort aux refractaires."* (The "refractory" priests—also called the "nonjuring" priests—referring to those who had refused to take the oath of loyalty to the new state or to deny their allegiance to the Catholic Church.) Before they were captured, the priests hid inside the church, behind the choir and the altar, some climbing the trees outside and fleeing into *rue Cassette* only to be captured in *Place Saint-Sulpice*.

The murders took three days. The corpses were left to rot in the courtyard and the garden. The macabre story of the September Massacres belongs to the history of the French Revolution.

Marie de' Medici founded the church in 1613; the interior remains as it was from the beginning: sweet and modest, with nothing triumphal about the architecture except the rise of the main altar against the rear north wall. Architecturally, it's put together in the Jesuit style, with Corinthian pillars and rich decorations—lovely paintings in many small chapels— and a classical pediment above the front entrance. Seen from the outside, it's a discreet church. You hardly notice it when you pass the entrance and the sign for the church on *rue de Vaugirard* (the longest street in Paris, stretching from *boulevard Saint-Michel* to the *Porte de Versailles*). *Carmes* is said to be the first Italian Baroque church in Paris. (Some historical plaques say it's the second.)

The night of the **Bataclan** massacre on November 13, 2015, I was walking with a friend down the hill of Oberkampf in the eleventh *arrondissement*. It was early, about nine o'clock. I was leaving the next morning to fly back to New York. I noticed as we walked that the usually loud and convivial cafés along *rue Oberkampf* were closed, that my friend Suzanne and I were the only people on the street. When we came to boulevard Richard-Lenoir, we stopped at a red light. I saw that Suzanne suddenly seemed alarmed; she was approaching a stranger on the corner and asking questions. I stood at the fence on the median of Lenoir looking into the darkness of the park that extends to Bastille. Suddenly a young man came running toward us from the direction of Bataclan, panting, crying, gasping, then holding onto the fence to keep himself on his feet. He sobbed and sobbed. He spat and choked and groaned. He seemed very sick, about to collapse. Standing behind him, I saw flashing lights coming from a line of police cars parked beyond the hedges.

Then the shooting started. Loud, nonstop, artillery flashing over the hedges, blasts of gunfire coming faster and faster and louder. Screaming. More screaming and screaming, more and more shots. Suzanne ran toward me, grabbed my arm, and pulled me back toward *Oberkampf.* I followed her across Lenoir, Oberkampf, and into a corner café. People were crouched on the floor, underneath the tables. We looked for a space but there was none. The man in charge told us to get out, we had come to the least safe place there was right now. Cafés were targets.

We ran back up the hill of *Oberkampf,* again the only people on the street. We ran without stopping to breathe until we turned into *République* and were soon inside the courtyard of my son's building. Suzanne said *terrorists.* By now, the sound of sirens seemed to have taken over the city, planes and helicopters the sky. I could still hear the gunfire. On TV, we saw reports: terrorists had invaded the northeast of Paris, especially the tenth and eleventh *arrondissements.*

All night, I kept hearing over and over the sound of the murders. Gunshots throughout the night. Cops? Terrorists? The terrorists were finishing off whoever was still alive, the cops were targeting terrorists. One hundred thirty-seven people were massacred that night, many more wounded. Body parts and pools of blood covered the floors of Bataclan and the sidewalks outside. A battlefield. The **Bataclan Massacre.**

At dawn I went back down *rue Oberkampf* to my hotel. Stores and cafés had been converted into hospitals, holding areas, *Centenaire* on *rue Oberkampf* and *rue Amelot,* the *Royale* across boulevard Beaumarchais, *Progres,* most streets taped off, my hotel still in lockdown, cops scrutinizing the IDs of ambulance drivers. I saw that Suzanne and I had been only half a block from Bataclan as we'd waited the night before for the light to change on Lenoir. Bataclan was a place I'd often passed, funky, large, neon, a lively bar scene, guest bands blasting music into the streets. I'd hoped to take in a concert some night.

On *rue Amelot,* across from my hotel, where Bataclan's rear entrance was, I saw on TV that survivors had jumped out of windows on the high floors in the rear of Bataclan. The images of flying bodies brought back the morning of 9/11 when I saw, from my apartment window in New York, the bodies of victims leaping and diving into flames and smoke—like gigantic crows on fire. Bodies on fire falling out the high windows of the World Trade Center.

That Saturday in Paris, *Le Monde* had its Bataclan edition in print by the time my plane took off from CDG. Long articles explaining logistics, the identities of the dead, of the terrorists, their other targets in the *Stade,* throughout the tenth and eleventh—*Charonne,* cafés mostly—long commentary on terrorism itself. (In World War II, more Jews were deported from and killed in the eleventh *arrondissement,* which held the largest Jewish community and number of *résistants* in Paris, than in any other.)

But terrorism in contemporary Paris? The *Charlie Hebdo* massacre I thought had been a fluke, in no way a pattern. Paris was and always will be the city of civilization, of taste and wit and sympathy.

I was forgetting history.

Le Monde made it sound unthinkable: nothing so horrible as the Bataclan Massacre had ever happened in Paris. As I read, what came to my mind were the religious wars between Protestants and Catholics in the sixteenth and seventeenth centuries: the Saint Bartholomew's Day Massacre, for instance, when fanatical Catholics murdered thousands of Protestants in Paris in a few nights and days, and approximately fifteen to twenty thousand in other cities. (See "Henri IV's Beautiful City," *The Streets of Paris*.) The Seine ran red. There were endless Wars of Religion in the decades preceding and following the Saint Bartholomew's Day Massacre, there was continuous torture of religious heretics. The French guillotined thousands following the seizure of the Bastille in 1789. The smell from the guillotine in Bastille reeked. During the Reign of Terror, from September 1793 until July 1794, the Committee of Public Safety, headed by Robespierre and Saint-Just, committed countless acts of savagery throughout Paris, in the *Champ-de-Mars*, the *Tuileries*; on the King's Swiss Guard; on prisoners, women, children, thieves, beggars, nobles, wealthy merchants, nonjuring priests. Twenty thousand people were guillotined. An Englishman recalled that as he came out of the Châtelet, he plunged up to his knees into rivers of blood.

When the Terror took a less bloody turn, so did the acts of religious repression. All churches were to be destroyed or converted to some secular purpose. Some were pulled down, though the mobs desecrated them before they disappeared: they burned the relics of Saint Geneviève on Place de Grève (see p. 44), stripped the carved woodwork from the church of **Saint-Gervais,** turned **Sainte Chapelle** (see p. 23) into a storehouse for flour and *Saint-Germain-des-Prés* into a gunpowder factory. The *Cathedral of Notre-Dame* became a Temple of Reason, where the Opera's corps de ballet performed a Dance of Reason in front of the high altar.

Inside *Carmes* these days, the serene beauty of its world remains. The frescoes are striking. In the west transept of the sanctuary, a delicate marble *statue of the Virgin and Child,* carved by the Italian Antonio Raggi to a design by *Bernini,* sits high, on the level of the main altar. There are signs of the Carmelite community that had occupied the church and convent since they—the Discalced (or Barefoot) Carmelites from Italy and followers of the Spanish Saint John of the Cross and Saint Teresa of Ávila—had arrived in Paris in 1611—for instance, paintings in honor of the prophet Elijah, carried up into heaven by a whirlwind, and the Carmelite saints Teresa and John of the Cross. The bones of the massacred priests are buried in the crypt. There is a Chapel of the Martyrs, their names incised in the walls, on the church's east side; another small chapel on the east (right) side as you face the main altar is dedicated to the memory of the nineteenth-century Sorbonne professor and social justice activist Frédéric Ozanam, who founded the Society of Saint Vincent de Paul, and organized many programs in Paris on behalf of the poor and homeless. (There are many low-income housing projects named for Ozanam in the western United States.)

In 1845 the Dominican order bought the buildings next door to the church, naming the complex the *Institut Catholique*, built in the Flemish neo-Gothic architectural style. It's one of the largest Catholic teaching institutions in Europe. It has a renowned past: on its faculty were Jacques Maritain; Édouard Branly; the paleontologist and theologian

Pierre Teilhard de Chardin (see p. 73) until he was fired by his conservative Jesuit superior, who found Teilhard's treatise on the "Cosmic Christ" unorthodox, if not heretical. If Teilhard had written two centuries earlier, we may never have known his work. (You can request a catalog and a schedule of summer courses inside at the admissions desk.)

The garden of the *institut,* just west of the church through a door off the *Saint-Joseph-des-Carmes'* courtyard, is lively with students enrolled in French language courses, especially on summer evenings. It's an easy place to relax under the plane trees and roses. But it's haunted. I wonder if the kids practicing their French or Urdu or Dutch have any idea of what happened here, if they've ever heard of the **September Massacres.**

Through the doorway that leads from this courtyard into the church courtyard, where we began this visit, in early winter you can see old people with canes, holding on to one another, the bowed, hunched parishioners of today's **Saint-Joseph-des-Carmes,** picking their steps across the icy cobblestones to enter the church for the six o'clock Mass. In November it's already dark and cold. On such evenings, the memory of the priests butchered on these stones is faint, but it's not gone. The violence of Paris's **Wars of Religion,** its centuries of culture wars—reenacted in November 2015—have left scars.

Nearby

LE PETIT LUXEMBOURG: *Two minutes across from **Saint-Joseph-des-Carmes** on the south side of **rue de Vaugirard and rue Férou,** the residence of the president of the French Senate. Often used as an exhibition space. An elegant building behind* *an ornate high black fence with a small chapel, an outdoor café in spring and summer, and magnificent flower beds.*

Related Reading

Christopher Hibbert, *The French Revolution*

Graham Robb, "Lost," in *Parisians: An Adventure History of Paris*

Matthew Cobb, *The Resistance: The French Fight Against the Nazis*

Notre-Dame du Travail

Montparnasse

NOTRE-DAME DU TRAVAIL

LOCATION: 59, RUE VERCINGÉTORIX
HOURS: Sun Masses: 9 (in Portuguese), 10:45; 6 (in
   Latin); weekdays, open 7:30–7:45; Sat, 9–7:30; Sun,
   8:30–7:30
MÉTRO: Pernety; Plaisance
WWW.NOTREDAMEDUTRAVAIL.NET/

It's a longish métro ride from my home away from home in northeastern Paris to western Montparnasse, but the out-of-the-wayness of the church of *Notre-Dame du Travail* has its rewards. This part of Montparnasse, the fourteenth *arrondissement*, is down-to-earth, off the tourist track. Small shops line the main drag, *rue Raymond Losserand.* You'll find fresh produce, *boucheries,* stationery, flowers, *pâtisseries,* charcuteries. A good bookstore: *Librairie Tropiques* at no. 63, well stocked in fiction and nonfiction (in French), crowded on weekends. *Rue des Thermopyles,* which cuts into the east side of the main street, has been called by locals the most beautiful street in Paris. It's charming like a movie set. (*Thermopyles* connects this part of the *quartier* with the area of Montparnasse where Alberto Giacometti lived and worked for forty years in his studio at *46, rue Hippolyte Maindron.*) (See *The Streets of Paris,* pp. 153–61.)

DIRECTIONS: As you exit the Pernety métro—the area is called *le village Pernety, a twenty-minute walk south of Saint Jean's Lutheran on rue de Grenelle*—bear left, heading west on *rue Pernety to rue Vercingétorix,* where the church is located. (At the corner, turn right and walk a few blocks north to no. 59). The walk from the métro to the church takes about ten minutes. (*Rue Vercingétorix* is named for the leader of the Gallic tribes that finally defeated Julius Caesar, the leader of the Gallic Wars, ending Caesar's Roman rule in Gaul [France] in 52 BCE.)

The church of *Notre-Dame du Travail* has a conventional Romanesque stone exterior, but once you enter, you understand straightaway why this church is considered so original. It is a masterpiece of metal architecture, made of iron and steel, built to look like a railroad station and, in parts, like a factory. Its purpose was to provide the workers of the district, who'd been crowded out of a nearby church, with a larger place of worship. The local workers—construction workers, for the most part—helped build the Eiffel Tower as well as the hall of the Universal Exhibition of 1900 and the *Gare Montparnasse.* The iron scraps left over from these construction sites were used in the construction of this church. That's what you're looking at when you explore it: the leftovers from the Eiffel Tower and the exhibition halls of 1900 and the *Gare Montparnasse* made into a church.

The architecture tells the story of the church's roots in the life of this working-class neighborhood.

The columns (or pillars or piers) rise up, thin and seemingly fragile, to touch the ceiling, just under the roof above the high glass windows. "We want light iron columns," said the pastor, "to terminate in thin ribs like the leaves of the palm." No more thick stone pillars blocking the congregation's view of the altar and the pulpit. There are thin struts and bolts, the piers appearing as I beams. There is light in this church. The ten pretty chapels lining the side aisles have stenciled floral lines, painted in lovely watercolors by artisans of the parish. They are dedicated to saints (Joseph, Francis of Assisi, Luc, Eliguis) cherished by parish workers who built this church once the Eiffel Tower was finished. The bright colors, the exuberance of the chapels' decorations—and some sugary pastel sweetness—make you feel you're in Naples, where the pastor was born. The small baptismal chapel in the rear of the church, to the right of the entrance, has a feeling. There's no tension here; you're not inside a hushed ecclesiastical monument. There are no guards keeping an eye on strangers, directing traffic.

There is no traffic. On my first visit, *Notre-Dame du Travail* was empty, except for one woman who hurried through the church toward the stairway leading down to the basement. I heard children's voices coming from downstairs. *"Ouvrières? Demain, une fête!"* (*Saturday is a big day here, lots of work*), the woman called from the stairwell.

Not only does the architecture of the church reflect the working lives of its first parishioners, its history belongs to the zeitgeist at the turn of the century: the construction was completed in 1902. Its founder and pastor was *Abbé Roger Soulange-Bodin,* born in Naples (1861), a French child, raised in Paris and in the seminary of nearby *Saint-Sulpice.* After his ordination his family wanted him assigned to a wealthy parish, Saint Augustine in the ninth *arrondissement,* but *Soulange-Bodin* insisted on a more popular apostolate in a poor parish, with all its misery. He was assigned in 1896 to build a new church for the workers of *le village Pernety.* This was the period of Social Catholicism, inspired by Pope Leo XIII's 1891 encyclical *De Rerum Novarum* ("Of New Things"), a kind of early New Deal condemning socialism but insisting on the Church's commitment to social justice, especially the rights of workers to form trade unions, to have decent housing, health care, and a just wage.

Rerum Novarum was always a matter of controversy in the Catholic Church.

Resistance to such a socialist-like manifesto marked the response not only of conservative political parties but of many conservatives in the Vatican and the wealthy congregations of Catholic Paris. *Abbé Soulange-Bodin* championed Social Catholicism as he had supported the syndicalism of that era, a radical current in the labor movement influenced by the French social philosophy of Pierre-Joseph Proudhon and Georges Sorel. It advocated transferring the ownership and control of the means of production and their distribution to the workers whose labor produced the society's wealth. *Syndicat* was the French word for trade union. The strike—*la grève*—was the primary method of protest against the injustices of capitalism and of gaining power for the working class.

Abbé Soulange-Bodin of the Church of *Notre-Dame du Travail* became a leading figure of Social Catholicism in Paris at the turn of the century. He supported syndicalism's transfer of power to workers' unions in an age of "power relations" between the Catholic Church and the French State. He wrote a book advocating training in economics and social policy for future priests.

The book was banned by the church. In 1909 the priest was reassigned. *Notre-Dame du Travail* lost its protector. He died in 1925. There is a nearby street named for him: *rue Roger Soulange-Bodin, fourteenth arrondissement* (two streets to the right of and behind the church as you approach it from the south).

*   *   *

Years later, during World War II and in the decades after the war, *Soulange-Bodin*'s ideological successors, known as the *Worker Priests of France,* realizing the estrangement between the church and the working classes derived from the systemic injustice of French society, also tried to establish new ways of serving the poor and at least challenging the exploitation of workers. (This was the era of *Abbé Pierre* and the creation of *Emmaus House.* See pp. 52, 55.) The priests took jobs in factories and coal mines; they built dams and roads. They made friends with their coworkers, usually keeping their identities as priests private. There was enthusiasm for such change among young priests. (See *Priest and Worker: The Autobiography of Henri Perrin.*) Some predicted that if the clergy did not get out of their rectories and parish halls, in fifty years the churches would be empty.

But the Vatican feared the taint of Communism within the labor movement as well as in the socialist politics embraced by Leo XIII and his ancestors: the prophets of early Christianity. *Democracy,* said Walt Whitman, has its roots in religion: "*Love thy neighbor in the New Testament has always been a part of the Democratic ideal.*"

In 1954, the Vatican banned the worker priests in France, under the threat of excommunication, just as it had suppressed the ministry of *Abbé Soulange-Bodin.* That was the end of the reform of the clergy. *Henri Perrin* (1914–1954), a Jesuit, died in a motorcycle crash before he could decide whether to resign from the priesthood or submit to Rome and leave the worker-priest movement.

The priests who submitted followed orders, imposed by Rome, picked up by local bishops. These days French churches are often (usually?) empty, except for scheduled liturgies and concerts.

Notre-Dame du Travail is at once a thrilling and sad place to visit. Though original and inviting in its architecture and art—and inspiring because of the story of its first pastor—it is also a kind of tomb where the idealism of young activists and priests of the early- to mid-twentieth century lies buried alive. On the Saturday when I dropped in, the pews were empty; children, supervised by one woman, could be heard having fun down in the basement.

But there is still in the dioceses of Paris and environs the right to protest against injustice: the *grève* remains legal and priests can still be seen marching alongside the workers. (Some Catholics celebrate the "Feast Day" of Father Henri Perrin: April 13.)

Nearby

HÔPITAL NECKER ENFANTS MALADES: *Paris's primary pediatric hospital. Exit **Notre-Dame du Travail**, bear right into **boulevard Montparnasse**, then at the next corner, turn left into **rue de Sèvres**. Midblock on the left is the public hospital named for Jacques Necker, French finance minister under Louis XVI and the father of the writer Madame de Staël.*

THE "TOWER"—*le **Tour**—of the American artist **Keith Haring** can be seen through the fence of the **Necker**. The sight and height of the **Tower** (almost ninety feet), its bright joyful shapes and colors—red, yellow, green, blue, with black graffiti—will knock your socks off. To get closer, enter the grounds through the hospital entrance lobby and walk to the rear of the hospital garden (with many benches), a ninety-seven-thousand-square-foot space planted in greens and yellows, a site of boundless gaiety. "I made this painting to amuse the sick children in this hospital, now and* in the future," Keith Haring (1958–1990) wrote in his diary in 1987 when he gave it to the city. It was restored in 2016 and installed here, with the support of the Keith Haring Foundation.

Keith Haring's art—"his cartoonish universe of dancing figures and barking dogs," as the New York Times described it— came out of the street and subway culture of New York City in the 1980s. One of his most famous works is the "Life of Christ" triptych, which includes the "Radiant Baby" (or the "Radiant Christ" or "Radiant Child"). The Haring Foundation gave it to the church of **Saint-Eustache** (see p. 141) in central Paris. His work was exhibited in Europe early in his career, in Paris at the Beaubourg (Centre Pompidou). He died of an AIDS-related illness at thirty-one.

Related Reading

Henri Perrin, *Priest and Worker: The Autobiography of Henri Perrin,* trans. Bernard Wall

Thomas Bokenkotter, *Church and Revolution*

Pietro di Donato, *Christ in Concrete*

Saint-Jean Lutheran

SAINT-JEAN LUTHERAN

LOCATION: 147, RUE DE GRENELLE

HOURS: Sun, 10:30

> The hours of **Saint-Jean** are erratic. They're posted at the front gate, on a glass-covered bulletin board. The Sunday liturgy is pretty regular—at 10:30—but weekday events change. As of this writing, the church is open for prayer every Tuesday at 12:45. But check the website for updates. Besides the schedule of services, the church offers a selection of parish activities: www.paroise-lutherienne-saintjean.org.

MÉTRO: La Tour-Maubourg

DIRECTIONS: The Protestant Lutheran church of **Saint-Jean** in Paris is located near the southwest corner of **rue de Grenelle** just across **boulevard de La Tour-Maubourg** and the garden in honor of **Antoine de Saint-Exupéry** *on* **Square Santiago du Chili.** As you walk west along **rue de Grenelle,** the church is on your left.

A delightful surprise: the small church set back from the sidewalk at the corner of *Grenelle,* more like a chapel out of a beautifully illustrated storybook—as you approach it from the street, you feel as if you're entering a botanical garden nestled into an urban forest though any touch of "urban" seems far, far away. The garden surrounds you on both sides, so rich in the darkest, brightest, densest green; the tall majestic trees rising into the sky, high above the lovely gardens covering the grounds and pressing the colors of their flowers—begonia, azalea, roses—into the wall of green. A narrow path winds around the church building, taking you into a back garden with benches.

Whoever designed this church and its setting was clearly enchanted with Nature: this church and its garden—its abundance of trees—are demonstrations of love, if not adoration.

The emphasis of the various liturgies at *Saint Jean*'s and its outreach programs are ecumenical, which means that different church traditions work together to develop closer relationships and stronger unity. The goal of ecumenism, emphasized at the Catholic Vatican Council of 1963–65, is to create one Christian family. It is also to work and worship together with Jews and Muslims. So, in accordance with this goal, the choir of *Saint-Jean* Lutheran sings with the Catholic choir of *Saint-Merri* on Thursday nights at 8 and at weekend concerts (see p. 149) with other choirs at *Saint-Merri*. Lutheran pastors share the pulpits in Catholic churches, for example at *Saint-Pierre du Gros-Caillou* on *rue Saint-Dominique*. *Saint-Jean* Lutheran also shares a global mission with other congregations on the Left Bank and throughout the world to oppose torture; together they form a united community of prayer, study, communication, and protest.

Taizé prayer takes place weekly (though that schedule is not regular since the onset of Covid). It's an ecumenical worship service created by a monastic community of Protestant and Catholic monks in Burgundy in 1940. It includes the singing of simple chants, scriptural prayers, and readings, often with candles and interludes of silence, which originated in *Taizé, Burgundy,* about 380 miles from Paris. *Taizé* prayer takes place in local churches all over the world. (In Paris, in

Saint-Germain-des-Prés [p. 77], and in several churches in New York City and the United States).

The music and history of *Johann Sebastian Bach, Lutheran,* is studied and performed at *Saint-Jean* **Lutheran.** Feast days are celebrated with music as well as sumptuous-looking communal suppers served in the gardens to a diverse gathering.

Inside the church, a striking architectural simplicity creates a very different atmosphere from the decorated and ornate churches of Catholicism or the synagogues of Judaism. The organ is smaller than Catholic organs; the main aisle is narrow; the altar is modest and recessed, not prominent. There is only the occasional statue. The very simplicity casts a spell: the music of this church and the tone of the sermons and psalms that are recited and sung suggest the plainness of dogma and the kindness of heart that is the aspiration of this community. The physical simplicity also reflects the slant of reforms delivered to Christianity by Luther and Calvin. Instead of the emphasis on an elaborate liturgy and the traditional Catholic themes of the Fall and redemption, nature and grace, sin and sacraments, Protestant theology and worship were lean. You don't find complicated theological distinctions about the influence of Saint Thomas Aquinas or Augustine or Francis of Assisi. Both sects, however, have sin and evil in their mind's eye. Both are haunted by it.

But a merciful Jesus is the focus of Protestantism. It doesn't seem to come apart over whether he's divine or human or a bit of both.

To look back at the history of Protestantism in Paris as it struggled to become an accepted part of Catholic France requires a strong stomach. The Wars of Religion in France (1562–1598), in which three million people died, cast traditional Catholicism against the new versions of Christianity that came in with the Protestant Reformation in the sixteenth century: the Calvinists of John Calvin, Martin Luther's Lutherans, Henry VIII's Anglicans, and other reformers. The bloodshed and the brutal atrocities of this combat make it the second deadliest religious war in European history. Pregnant women had their bellies sliced open, their babies removed and cut to pieces; corpses and body parts glutted the streets: the Seine ran red, rats ran everywhere.

The Catholics considered the Protestants heretics; they burned them alive in *Place de Grève* when they caught them. The Protestants detested the corruption of the Church in Rome, the idea that a sinner or the pope could sell one's way into heaven or buy yourself out of purgatory by means of indulgences. They saw many examples of Catholic idolatry and superstition. Protestants, for example, did not believe in the Real Presence of the body and blood of Jesus in the Eucharist; they spoke of "symbolism"; Catholics, according to Protestants, believed they were eating human flesh in the sacrament of the Eucharist. More heresy in their eyes.

And Catholic Paris would not tolerate a Protestant king, one Henri Navarre, Protestant, who was next in line to the French throne in 1589. When, at the height of the war, Henri Navarre, the *vert galant* whose mother was Protestant, capitulated and converted to Catholicism for the sake of inheriting the throne in Catholic France and bringing an end to the Wars of Religion, Catholic Paris allowed him to be crowned as the Catholic King Henri IV. At least the war(s) were over. (Not really: there were twenty-three assassination attempts on Henri's life after his coronation, most of them by Jesuits.) And many staunch Catholics did not trust King Henri's conversion. It was fake, according to purists. For example, as king—"*Good King Henri*"—granted clemency, issuing the **Edict of Nantes** (1598), which allowed the Huguenots to worship in some public places and hold office:

> *Those who honestly follow their conscience are of my religion, and as for me, I belong to the faith of all those who are gallant and good....*

The Catholic Sun King, Louis XIV, revoked this act of tolerance in 1685, and Protestants, fearing a resumption of the Wars of Religion, left France for safer havens in Europe and America. They left behind a country that, in spite of all that had happened—the torture and the agony and the wars between both sects—was still overwhelmingly Catholic.

These days, the sane among religious believers have gotten more used to a pluralistic society. Lutherans worship with Catholics, Catholics with Lutherans. Anglicans worship with everybody. Non-Jews are welcomed in Jewish synagogues, especially at such religious ceremonies as Bar Mitzvahs. (Roman Catholics are not as strong in numbers as they were in the sixteenth century. They comprise only 60 percent of religious observers, Protestants 3 percent; 28 percent of Parisians have no religious affiliation. Jews number approximately four hundred thousand in religious Paris.)

Catholic and Protestant Christians as well as Jews are united in their respect for the memory of the Lutheran pastor and martyr **Dietrich Bonhoeffer** (1906–1945), who was murdered by the Nazis at Flossenbürg for his role in the underground that tried to assassinate Hitler. Bonhoeffer was convinced it was his duty as a Christian to work for Hitler's defeat. He spent two years in prison in Germany, knowing execution was in his future; the Hebrew Psalms were the prayers that gave him most strength. The most important of the many books of theology he left behind are the extraordinary *Letters and Papers from Prison* and *The Cost of Discipleship*. And perhaps the most quoted passage from Bonhoeffer's theology in all Lutheran churches—and in other Protestant denominations, Catholicism, and Judaism—is his reference to

> *our relation to God as a new life in existence for others. . . .*
> *The transcendental is not infinite and unattainable tasks,*
> *but the neighbor who is within reach in any given situation.*

Bonhoeffer urged his followers in Europe to work for justice in the here and now, for the losers, the forgotten, the silenced. That is the witness of **Saint-Jean** Lutheran on rue de Grenelle. That is the witness of Jewish believers, who are committed to "repairing the world" (*tikkun olam*), and of Catholics—at **Saint-Merri,** for example—who interpret Jesus as "the man for others."

"*Love is what you **do**,*" said **Abbé Pierre**. The Protestant Bonhoeffer and the Catholic Abbé Pierre and countless rabbis (Stephen Wise and Abraham Joshua Heschel in New York City come immediately to mind): in the twentieth century and into the twenty-first, they created and shared common ground.

Nearby

CAFÉ ROUSSILLON: *186, rue Cler. Wonderful beyond all telling. A good bistro with excellent food and service. Crowded and lively at lunchtime.*

SQUARE SANTIAGO DU CHILI: **boulevard de La Tour-Maubourg** *and* **rue de Grenelle.** *Cross the boulevard de La*

Tour-Maubourg and the lawns of the Esplanade of Les Invalides. You face the gleaming Église du Dôme. It's an oasis of peace with benches on a summer morning. The bust of **Saint-Exupéry** *(1900–1944) is lovely above a ring of flowers: he was one of France's first professional pilots as well as one of her most beautiful writers.* Wind, Sand and Stars; Night Flight; The Little Prince. *He was shot down by the Nazis in the Mediterranean, near Marseille.*

AMERICAN UNIVERSITY OF PARIS: *5, boulevard de La Tour-Marbourg, 75007, www. aup.eu. Near the Eiffel Tower and the Seine. Twenty-five undergrad majors, six fields of grad courses. All classes in English.*

CHURCH OF SAINTE-CLOTILDE: *Between* **rue Grenelle** *(walking east) and* **23 bis, rue las Cases.** *www.sainte-clotilde .com.On Square Samuel Rousseau. A lovely French Gothic revival, with two famous spires and superb choral concerts. César Franck, organist, 1859–1890. Métro: Solférino.*

THE EIFFEL TOWER: *Walk west along* **Grenelle,** *for about ten minutes until you reach the* **Seine. Tour Eiffel** *stands close to the river, on Quai Branly. It was adored and despised when it appeared in 1889, marking the centenary of the Revolution; it is now beloved. Gustave Eiffel (1832–1923) was the engineer, also despised and adored for his masterwork.*

Related Reading

Dietrich Bonhoeffer, *Letters and Papers from Prison*

Michael Marissen, *Bach & God*

Martin Marty, *The Christian World*

Russian Orthodox Cathedral of Saint Alexander Nevsky

RUSSIAN ORTHODOX CATHEDRAL OF SAINT ALEXANDER NEVSKY

LOCATION: RUE DARU

HOURS: Tues, Fri, Sun, 3–6

MÉTRO: Ternes; Courcelles

DIRECTIONS: Walk from the Place des Ternes exit, east along boulevard de Courcelles. Cross the wide street— you can see the cathedral from boulevard de Courcelles, large and splendid at the head of *rue Daru*.

There is such beauty and peace here. As you enter, you feel you have entered the soul of Russia. A few visitors, reverent, silent. Splendid Russian icons abound. Candelabra with many candles light the shadows and the faces of the saints in the icons.

Icons are paintings on wood, often small, though some found in churches and monasteries, such as this one, are much larger. There is an elaborate religious symbolism associated with them. The famous icon by Andrei Rublev (c. 1360s–1427) depicts the Trinity—the Catholic belief in a triune God: Father, Son, and Holy Spirit.

In Russian churches and in the Cathedral of *Saint Alexander Nevsky,* the nave is typically separated from the sanctuary by an iconostasis, or icon screen, a wall of icons with double doors in the center.

Icons represent the Gospel in paint, similar to the function of the stained glass windows in churches and cathedrals that tell the stories of the Old and New Testaments in colored and designed pieces of glass. Careful attention is paid by the iconographer to make sure that the Gospel stories and characters are faithfully drawn and conveyed. They are considered mystical objects, suggesting a vision has been experienced in the making of this art.

Some icons were considered miraculous. A true icon is looked upon as a gift from heaven, a painting opening the way to the Godhead, an icon able to perform miracles.

The Cathedral of **Saint Alexander Nevsky** was built here around 1847, when Russian Paris established itself in the northwest after large immigrations from Russia in the mid-nineteenth century. Russian aristocrats and leaders of industry had a history of doing business with France; the aristocratic Russians were fluent in the French language and devoted to French culture. The eighth *arrondissement,* where the cathedral is located, rich in Old World decorum and property values, suited their tastes and business interests.

The cathedral is named for the beloved Russian saint *Alexander Nevsky,* a military man and diplomat who saved the Russian lands of the western and eastern borders from invasion and conquest by the Teutonic (German) knights and the Swedes, whom he defeated in 1240 at the mouth of the Neva River. His surname comes from that place: Neva/Nevsky. Alexander, a brilliant statesman, also saved Russia from conquest by the Mongols with diplomacy and a certain humanity unusual for that time.

He was noted not only for his military leadership and statesmanship but also for his defense of Russian Orthodoxy in the West and his profound Christianity. He was unusual in all the roles he played: a ruler beloved by the Russian people.

He was canonized a saint in 1547. Hymns in his honor are still sung at religious services:

KONTAKION

We honor you as a most radiant, spiritual star,
Rising up from the east; going down in the west!
As you enriched the Russian people with good works and
miracles,
So now enlighten us who remember you in faith, O
Blessed Alexander.
Today as we celebrate your falling asleep, we ask you to
beseech the Lord
That He may strengthen his suffering servants and save
all Orthodox Christians!

Alexander's story is the subject of *Alexander Nevsky* (1938), the great Russian epic film by Sergei Eisenstein, its plot a kind of response to the current events of the time: the threat of Nazi invasion and domination of Europe and Russia. Stalin loved the film, until he didn't—the Nazi-Soviet Pact changed his mind for a time in one direction, then another. But Eisenstein survived the waves of Stalin's moods, and so did Sergei Prokofiev, who wrote the score. (Cantata *Alexander Nevsky* has been called "one of his greatest works" by Leopold Stokowski.) The film still plays in art houses and is part of the Criterion Collection of great classic films. And **Saint Alexander Nevsky** is still beloved, evident in the piety of the Russian congregants and choruses on Sundays.

The guides who circulate in the cathedral are extremely knowledgeable and friendly.

* * *

The small gardens outside make a lovely setting in season for this superb church under its spires and towers. *Rue Daru* leads from the cathedral in many directions. Within less than half an hour you can walk to Parc Monceau, Avenue Hoche, Salle Pleyel (see p. 143, *Hidden Gardens of Paris*), Musée Jacquemart-André, a number of these destinations representing the cultural richness that drew aristocratic Russian immigrants to the area in the nineteenth century.

There was another Orthodox house of worship to the south, in the slums of Montparnasse, the mission of the Russian refugee *Mother Maria Skobtsova*. A member of a prosperous and aristocratic family in Russia, she had married twice, once to a Bolshevik, later to an anti-Bolshevik. She fled the chaos of the wars in 1923, arriving in Paris with her three children and becoming deeply immersed in caring for destitute Russian refugees whom she found in the slums, mental asylums, prisons. "Each person is the very icon of God incarnate in the world," she wrote. The renewal of Orthodoxy was a part of her mission; she took religious orders in 1932. Caught rescuing Jews when the Nazis invaded in 1940, she was arrested and sent to *Ravensbrück* concentration camp, where she died in 1945.

Nearby

LE DIPLOMATE: *An art deco café restaurant at 110, boulevard de Courcelles as you head southeast from the Ternes métro, toward the cathedral. French and European food, wine bar, beer, lively happy hour, friendly, and pretty.*

ARC DE TRIOMPHE: *About half a mile west from the cathedral, a visit and a site that establishes the ambiance of this quietly opulent neighborhood.*

PARC CLICHY BATIGNOLLES-MARTIN-LUTHER-KING: *A half-hour walk northeast from boulevard Courcelles, following boulevard Malesherbes and the signs. A newish park, good for skaters and visiting on the many benches with friends. Quiet, a real sanctuary. The restaurant Coretta, in the park, is a great treat.*

Related Reading

Sergei Hackel, *Pearl of Great Price: The Life of Mother Maria Skobtsova, 1891–1945*

Andrei Tarkovsky, *Andrei Rublev*

THE RIGHT BANK

Saint-Germain l'Auxerrois

SAINT-GERMAIN L'AUXERROIS

LOCATION: 2, PLACE DU LOUVRE; RUE DE L'AMIRAL DE
COLIGNY
HOURS: Tues–Sat, 9–7; Sun, 9:30–8:15
MÉTRO: Louvre-Rivoli; Pont Neuf

L*'Église Saint-Germain l'Auxerrois* on the Right Bank
rivals *L'Église Saint-Germain-des-Prés* on the Left as
one of the prettiest churches in Paris. It is also soaked in one
of the ugliest episodes in the history of Paris, a kind of holocaust, which could only have transpired with the pretty
church's complicity.

Auxerrois comes from the name of the city of *Auxerre* in
Burgundy where the red wine grape (Côt) is grown and is
part of the mix of grapes that became *Malbec*.

The church's patron saint, *Germanus,* a bishop of *Auxerre* who preached the ascetic life to the young *Saint Geneviève* (there's a painting of the two saints together on the
rear wall in the church of *Saint-Germain de Charonne* [see
p. 213]), is the same bishop who settled in fifth to sixth century Merovingian Paris. Since his time, there have been four
modifications to the church: a twelfth-century bell tower; a
thirteenth-century choir and central portal; a fourteenth-
century porch, nave, and transept; and sixteenth-century
side chapels and porches. (There was extensive destruction
to this church during the Revolution and the riots of 1831.)

The impression you get on entering *Auxerrois* is of a sweet
harmony of architecture and color and effects. (There's no

trace of Caesar's legions or the Viking raiders who once camped on this site.) In the Middle Ages this was the church of the royal family, whom Charles V moved out of the *Conciergerie* and into the *Palais du Louvre* in the late fourteenth century. There are distinct Gothic and Renaissance features, but all the parts appear together in a unified graceful elegance.

The church is double aisled, but it feels smaller—or more compact—than it is.

The highlight, to my mind, is the small chapel to the right of the entrance, the *Lady Chapel* (also called the thirteenth-century chapel of the Holy Sacrament) with an altarpiece in the form of a Tree of Jesse, which bears a fourteenth-century painted statue of a young and delicate *Virgin and Child*. Above it hangs a mural painting of the *Coronation of the Virgin*. The medallions in the distinctive stained-glass windows of the chapel bear motifs from the Hebrew Bible, images of sensual heroic women who in different ways resisted a patriarchal oppressive order: *Esther* in the first window; fearless *Judith* in the second, holding a sword and draped in turquoise, coral, and purple; and a brilliant, assured *Deborah* in the third window. Marguerite de Valois, daughter of François I, who would marry the *vert galant* Henri Navarre, attended Mass in this church regularly, a devout and scholarly princess who would dance through the night in the *Louvre Palace* ballrooms and spend her days reading Latin in the library. Fitting company for the bold Hebrew women prophets in this chapel's windows.

In the rear of the chapel, perpendicular to the rear south wall, is a statue of *Saint Germanus,* the confessor of *Saint Geneviève* and namesake of the church. On the south wall, near *Saint Germanus,* is a wooden sculpture identified as *Saint*

Mary of Egypt, a strange image of a large woman, wrapped in her own hair. Her story is strange, too. According to the legendary account of her life in the *Catholic Encyclopedia,* she was a prostitute and, as such, is the patron saint of female penitents. (Did all female penitents start out as prostitutes?)

Born in 344, she left home in Alexandria at the age of twelve, worked as a prostitute for seventeen more years, then joined a pilgrimage to Jerusalem in search of more customers. There, at the door of a church, she met a priest/monk named Zosimus who would later give her Holy Communion after she repented her past life. She left the pilgrimage and headed into the Palestine desert and Arabia. A year later Zosimus returned and found her almost a skeleton. A true penitent, she had survived on herbs in the desert. (Though her statue in *Saint-Germain l'Auxerrois* captures a large-hipped big-bellied woman carrying three large loaves of bread.) A year later, in 421, Zosimus returned to the desert where he found her corpse, which he buried.

Why she is venerated in Paris may seem mysterious. Perhaps because Paris is a city of many fictional prostitutes who, as expressed by the pens of their male authors, starve and repent and suffer as they lay dying. Their deaths are punishments, presumably for their uncontrolled sins of lust. Henri Murger's Mimi in *Scènes de la vie de Bohème* and the title character of Émile Zola's *Nana* exemplify the pattern: the whore who died of sinful lust and finally of starvation.

(This statue, however, also recalls one of a naked *Saint Mary Magdalene* [1510] in painted lime wood. "Her nakedness," according to the *Blue Guide to Paris,* refers to the legend of the Magdalen living as a mystic ascetic in a cave in Sainte-Baume [Provence] clothed only in her hair.)

As you walk around the church, you pass more objects

that present stark juxtapositions to the pious narratives told by other holy objects.

On the south side of the church, above a doorway near the beginning of the ambulatory, is the adorable *Vierge à l'oiseau* (Virgin with a bird), a fifteenth-century wooden sculpture of a small bird perched on the Virgin's arm as she holds out a piece of food to it. Then, from the sweetness of these images, you pass on to the north side of the ambulatory, where you find an altarpiece of the *Passion,* with the Crucifixion, the Way of the Cross, and a fainting Virgin in relief. The story of Holy Week: torture, murder, burial, sorrow.

The exterior of the church, as seen from a wide front porch bordered by a median of tulips and trees, faces a bell tower—*the belfry of Saint-Germain*. The church bell's name is *"La Mairie."* It rang out the night of August 24, 1572, to signal the start of the *Saint Bartholomew's Day Massacre*. It triggered the slaughter of Huguenots in the streets and court-yards of the city. The *Louvre Palace* saw Catholic soldiers throwing spears and swords and daggers, clogging its halls with the dead and wounded. The Catholics hit their targets; the thousands of Protestant wedding guests who'd come to Paris to witness the marriage of the Catholic *Reine Margot* to the Protestant *Henri of Navarre* were trapped. The Protestant guests, bedded down in the Louvre, jumped out the windows into the courtyards to escape.

The sacrament of royal matrimony, it had been thought, would mark the end of the bloody religious/civil wars of the sixteenth century, it would herald the reconciliation of Catho-lics and Protestants. Instead, the bodies of the heretics were torn to pieces, corpses thrown into the Seine. The river ran red. The bridegroom hid in a closet, as the story goes, with the help of his new bride. Years later, Henri IV, after renouncing his Protestant faith and becoming a Catholic king (see p. 114) issued the *Edict of Nantes* (1598), which granted freedom of religion (or worship in restricted places) to Protestants. But in 1685, the Catholic Bourbon King Louis XIV revoked it. Thousands of Huguenots, remembering the Valois–Navarre wedding reception—*ding-dong bell, heretics in the well*—emigrated to the New World, to Geneva, northern Europe, and the Atlantic city of La Rochelle (see p. 135).

These days the bell tower of the *Auxerrois church* gives a Wednesday *carillon* concert (1:30–2:00) of Bach, Couperin, Mozart. There are benches outside for sitting and listening to the music. Since the fire that so severely damaged the *Cathedral of Notre-Dame* on April 15, 2019, the cathedral clergy have been using *Saint-Germain l'Auxerrois*, which once ministered to the royalty of the *Louvre Palace* for Christmas services.

Is it possible that ten to fifteen thousand Protestants died that night in 1572 when the *"Maire"* sounded? The next day the Pope sent a golden rose in tribute to the Catholic king and his mother, Catherine de' Medici, when, to celebrate the slaughter of heretics, a Te Deum was sung in Rome, when the victorious Wars of Religion recruited thousands more troops and treaties of peace never materialized.

Paris is now secular Paris; Protestants and Catholics keep the peace. But the clash of diverse religions and national identities is still a source of mayhem. The memory of massacres lingers in contemporary Paris in the echoes of *Je suis Charlie* on the boulevards.

Nearby

"THE SAINT," A MEDIEVAL SCULPTURE IN THE LOUVRE: *Open daily except Tues, 9–5:45; Weds and Fri until 9:45. To avoid lines, buy tickets at FNAC or online, www.louvre.fr/.* **Exit the métro at Louvre/Palais Royale** *or walk straight across the street from Auxerrois, through the* **Cour Carrée,** *to enter the museum at the Pyramid.* **(Follow the signs.)** *Ask for a map and directions at Information on the lower level. Walk up to Room 11 in the "French Sculpture 500–1500" section, in the* **Richelieu wing.** *It's a confusing search. Guard Catherine Kern-RanVat from Brittany helped me find this exquisite sculpture: a young woman, carved in alabaster, a soft creamy white stone from the western French Alps, reading in utter stillness. Named "The Saint" by the art critic from the* New York Times, *Nicholas St. Fleur.*

MUSÉE DE L'ORANGERIE: *Weds–Mon 9–6; closed Tues. www .musee-orangerie.fr. Bookshop and shop. At the far end (west) of the* **Tuileries,** *on the south side. Descending to the lower level of the museum, you will find yourself wrapped round by the panels of Claude Monet's* **Les Nymphéas (Water Lilies).** *This is one of those visions created by a great artist you will never forget. The effect of the reflected light of Monet's water, his colors—the blue of "Morning"—embodies a sense of infinity. Monet was drawn to Buddhism and the practice of contemplation. His later paintings were exhibited in such recent shows as* Mystical Landscapes *and* Au-dela des Étoiles. *At the Musée Marmottan Monet (Tues–Sun, 10–6; Thurs, 8; closed Mon, at the west side of the Ranelagh gardens) are ninety-four Monet canvases, the largest collection in the world.*

LE FUMOIR: **6, rue de l'Amiral de Coligny.** *Three minutes north from Saint-Germain l'Auxerrois. On the corner next to/north of the Mairie. Good food and ambiance. Just across from the* **Louvre.** *Reserve. www.lefumoir.com.*

Related Reading

Christine de Pisan, *The Treasure of the City of Ladies*

Alexandre Dumas, *La Reine Margot*

Ross King, *Mad Enchantment: Claude Monet and the Painting of the Water Lilies*

André Maurois, *A History of France*

Notre-Dame des Victoires

NOTRE-DAME DES VICTOIRES

LOCATION: 6, RUE NOTRE-DAME DES VICTOIRES

HOURS: Mon–Fri, 7:00 and 12:10; Sat, 7:00; Sat Vigil, 5:15; Sun, 7:30, 9:00, 10:30, and 12:15

MÉTRO: Bourse; Palais Royal

WWW.NOTREDAMEDESVICTOIRES.COM/

Travelers, like everyone else, have multiple identities and some weird tastes. In the space defining *Notre-Dame des Victoires,* inside and out, there's history, beauty, idiosyncrasy, meanness of spirit—something for every variety of visitor.

At first glance, after leaving the *Palais Royal* at its north end and bearing right into *rue de Beaujolais* and then straight along into the lovely *Place des Petits-Pères,* there is the image of a friendly church square, benches half framing the entrance porch, a few people and couples sitting, nestling, singles reading or looking up at the sky, kids practicing in-line skating, parents coaching. It's a good people-watching place, no shouty voices. Some days it's empty, except for a few cats.

On the eastern perimeter, an equestrian statue shows King Louis XIII (1601–1643) high in his saddle, waving, proud of his royal self as the horse beneath him lunges. Bronze horse and triumphal king are doing a kind of dance in celebration of the royal army's victory over the Protestants (Huguenots) in the western Atlantic seaport city of La Rochelle. The Siege of La Rochelle (1627–1628), led by

Cardinal Richelieu, lasted for fourteen months as the army and navy blockaded the prosperous Protestant port on the Bay of Biscay, trying to starve the heretical citizenry into defeat and ruin their seafaring economy. King Louis had prayed to the Blessed Virgin Mary to help him conquer La Rochelle's Protestant infidels. The Virgin came through. The king won. Catholic France: *Salut!*

Louis ordered a church, ***Notre-Dame des Victoires,*** to be built in thanksgiving. He laid the cornerstone in 1629, but because money ran out, the church wasn't completed until 1737.

It was soon famous as the church of thanksgiving. Pilgrims and parishioners decorated the interior walls, from floor to ceiling, with **ex-voto** plaques and candles. The name comes from the Latin *"ex voto suspepto,"* "the vow made." One section of candlelit petitions is filled with carved metal hearts, in silver and gold, engraved with names and prayers. An example: *"La Sainte Vierge Ma Conserve Mon Petit Garçon En Mai 1856. C and R"* ("May the Holy Virgin Save My Little Boy, May 1856. From C and R"—his parents' initials).

What you see as you enter the church today are more than thirty-seven thousand plaques and flickering votive candles. It's a dazzling blaze of pious gratitude that brightens the whole church up to the main altar. The carved dark mahogany woodwork of the choir around the altar makes an especially beautiful impression inside this surround of warm white light. (The facial expression of the statue of Our Lady of Victoire, high above the main altar—under the *Refugium Peccatores*—triumphal, like Louis on his horse, has a distinctly French hauteur beneath her bejeweled crown.) In her church, ***Notre-Dame des Victoires*** is more conqueror than comforter.

During the Nazi Occupation of 1940–1944, ordinary Parisians of all persuasions visited and left their petitions with their votive lights. The writer Colette (1873–1954), who lived nearby in the *Palais Royal* (the place she called a "village"), said the most crowded road out of the *Palais Royal* led to *Notre-Dame des Victoires*. She identified herself as a "pagan Catholic" or more prosaically as an agnostic, and compared this church to the village fountain where all the thirsty come to drink. In a large side chapel, Colette lit candles for friends, soldiers, and the *résistants*, who included her daughter.

In previous decades (and centuries), other parishioners and visitors to this church, some of whom became famous or canonized, included the musician Jean-Baptiste Lully (a parishioner who is buried here); the Curé of Ars; Saint Thérèse of Lisieux; Cardinal John Henry Newman, who came to give thanks for his conversion; the novelist Georges Bernanos (*The Diary of a Country Priest*) and student of Henri de Gaulle, the schoolteacher father of Charles de Gaulle; filmmaker Robert Bresson (1901–1999); *Abbé Pierre* (1912–2007, see pp. 52–56); Édith Piaf in 1937 and 1940; and, on September 1, 1944, five days after the Liberation, Charles de Gaulle.

Internationally beloved but little known as one of the famous pilgrims to this church is Wolfgang Amadeus Mozart (1756–1791), who spent half of 1778 living in abject poverty in *rue du Sentier* with his mother, Anna Maria (see *Nearby*). Mozart's ambition was to ingratiate himself as Salzburg's twenty-two-year-old wunderkind with music-loving Paris. (He was broke and needed cash.) He did produce his Paris Symphony (K. 297 in D major) in September of that year, two months after his mother died in his arms. Paris loved the symphony.

But Paris never embraced Mozart himself. French snobbery found Mozart's spontaneity, practical jokes, and

frivolity off-putting, his humanitarianism and tolerance perhaps an embarrassment, a sign of an inconsistent or capri-
cious character. Though he made anticlerical jokes, he did
not find Masonry incompatible with his Catholicism. In his
letters he refers to visiting his parish church, *Notre-Dame des
Victoires*. Following the premier of his Paris Symphony, he
visited the *Palais Royale*; had an ice (*glace*), as he told his diary; and then he went to *"Notre-Dame des Victoires as I had
promised, and said my chapelet (rosary)."* In 1778, the year of
his mother's death, he began to study the church music of
Bach. His first biographer wrote that "Church music was actually what Mozart was most fond of, but it was the variety
of music he had the least opportunity to write." When he returned to Salzburg, he and his music were thought to have
matured after the unhappy time he'd spent in Paris. In the
shadows of his mother's death and his failure to connect with
the people of Paris, he had had to grow up.

Nearby

8, RUE DU SENTIER: *"Maison Mozart" is a ten-minute walk
from the church, north toward the Bourse and then to the right
along rue Réaumur and left onto Sentier. Mozart and his mother
lived here in 1778.*

PALAIS ROYAL: *Colette's residence (see* The Streets of Paris,
*pp. 179–88) and Mozart's retreat. Exit through the north end—
you're right around the corner from the church—and explore their
neighborhood, starting across* **rue de Beaujolais,** *where you'll find
the charming passage of* **Galerie Vivienne** *at* **6, rue Vivienne**
and inside the excellent antiquarian bookstore **Librairie Jous-
seaume.**

BIBLIOTHÈQUE NATIONALE DE FRANCE, SITE RICHE-LIEU: *Exit the Palais Royal through the south end, turn right and right again into* **rue de Richelieu.** *Enter the courtyard of the library at* **58, rue de Richelieu.** *Entrance to the right across the courtyard. The Reading Room shows the ironwork of architect/engineer Henri Labrouste. One of the most beautiful rooms in Paris. (See p. 41, the "Nearby" to Saint-Étienne-du-Mont in the Latin Quarter.)*

Related Reading

Paul Johnson, *Mozart: A Life*

Peter Gay, *Mozart*

Saint-Eustache

SAINT-EUSTACHE

LOCATION: 2, IMPASSE SAINT-EUSTACHE; 146, RUE RAM-
   BUTEAU
HOURS: Mon–Fri, 9:30–7; weekday Masses, 12:30 and
   6; Sat, 6; Sun, 9:30 and 11 with organ and Saint-
   Eustache choir; Sun, 5:30, free organ concert
MÉTRO: Les Halles; Châtelet
WWW.SAINT-EUSTACHE.ORG

Sensational on the outside, or if you prefer, wildly Gothic as you come upon it from where the central markets had once been. The "belly of Paris," Zola called them. As you enter the church of *Saint-Eustache*—the church of *Les Halles*—you might feel a brooding gloom in the chilly stone vastness, the soaring nave reaching toward the arched roof. Then you walk around *Saint-Eustache*. Taking your time, you come upon treasure in all its stunning variety. *"A wonderful jumble,"* someone called it.

Entering *Saint-Eustache* when music is in motion and the sun is shining through the high stained glass windows on the south side, you might feel the vibrations of practicing choirs, or choral concerts caught in the play of light, or in the organ auditions, a rock band practicing, or the National Orchestra of France, its hundreds of instruments and voices celebrating, say, the Mass of Saint Cecilia, the patron saint of music. Every year on November 22, the vastness of *Saint-Eustache* seems to tremble with the power of singing in honor of the Roman Cecilia. Secular Paris is also faithful to her anniversary. Music is mostly what this church does (as Berlioz and Mozart and Liszt knew).

On June 5, 2019, the eve of the seventy-fifth anniversary of D-Day, 1944, the National Orchestra of France and its choir of several hundred male and female voices performed Johannes Brahms's German Requiem: the acoustics of *Saint-Eustache* supported the Requiem's celestial effects. The audience cooperated: as at most sacred concerts in Paris, there's not a cough or a cell phone destroying the peace.

Here and there, as you continue walking, *Saint-Eustache* strikes you as a museum. There's a sales area—a Welcoming Table—as you enter through the southeast door coming from *Les Halles*. Books, guides, cards, even a docent. Walking west along a south aisle toward the main western doorway where the eight-thousand-pipe organ presides—said to be "the largest pipe organ in France"—you pass a large folding display of information (the church was started in 1532 and consecrated in 1637) and pictures of the featured musical geniuses whose lives and music unfolded here and in this neighborhood. Rameau; Mozart, participating in his mother's funeral Mass in 1778; Lully, competitive and greedy, getting married here. Berlioz conducted the first performance of his Te Deum (1855) in *Saint-Eustache*, accompanied by 950 musicians. Liszt conducted his *Messe Solennelle* here.

The many side chapels in the north and south aisles show paintings in honor of saints (Geneviève, Agnès, the "Martyrdom of Saint Eustace"—the saint for whom the church is named was a Roman general of the second century who was burned alive with his family after he converted to Christianity). *The Supper at Emmaus* by Rubens or his school (1611) in the north chapel is the most precious painting in the church. (An *Emmaus* painting also appears in *Saint-Séverin* [see p. 33], **Saint-Merri** [see p. 149], and the **Louvre**.) Other paintings honor the workmen and tradesmen of **Les Halles**: fishmongers, orange sellers, egg merchants, vendors of secondhand clothes.

The sculptures include Pigalle's *Virgin* (1748) on the altar of the Lady Chapel at the church's eastern end. To the left of the Lady Chapel is the tomb of Jean-Baptiste Colbert, incorruptible secretary to Louis XIV (reigned 1643–1715). Further along in another north side chapel is the contemporary sculpture by Raymond Mason, *Le Demanagement des Halles* (1971), a foodie's Noah's ark commemorating the exodus of the city's beloved **Les Halles** markets out to Rungis near Orly, on February 28, 1969. In a nearby chapel is Keith Haring's triptych *Life of Christ*, in bronze and white gold, bringing to mind his "Radiant Child" towering over the children's hospital in Montparnasse (see p. 108).

The great French dramatist, actor, and author Jean-Baptiste Poquelin, baptized in **Saint-Eustache** in 1622, grew up around **Les Halles,** playing on the **Pont Neuf,** going to a Jesuit school, and joining a theater troupe when he was twenty against his father's wishes. (His mother died when he was ten.) **Saint-Eustache** was his parish church. When he became an actor, he was excommunicated. (The theater was a profession forbidden to Catholics for its representation of immorality; as such, excommunication was "a punitive action; a favorite device for . . . cutting off offenders from fellowship with the Christians in a particular place," as Diarmaid MacCulloch explains in *Christianity: The First Three Thousand Years*.) Poquelin changed his birth/baptismal name to his stage name: **Molière**. He was a gifted actor and prolific author who went south with his traveling theater troupe for about thirteen years.

Returning to Paris, Molière was able to land a stage and audience space first in the *Louvre* and then in the *Palais Royal* because of his on-again, off-again friendship with Louis XIV. King Louis loved comedy: the comic inventiveness and the underlying moral seriousness of Molière's vision moved him. He supported Molière's plays, though the playwright was attacked by his many prudish enemies and rivals. In his plays Molière created characters of hilarious and profound religious hypocrisy (*Tartuffe*); pedantry and hypochondria (*Le Misanthrope*); fake piety (*Le Bourgeois gentilhomme*); and the pretentiousness of young women in the salons (*Les Précieuses ridicules*). The beautiful and intelligent courtesan Ninon de l'Enclos of *rue des Tournelles* in the Marais (see *The Streets of Paris*, pp. 243–45), who scorned organized religion, was one of Molière's closest friends, enjoying in particular his trenchant anticlerical slant. The Church was not a fan of either Ninon or her famous friend. Both did jail time, Ninon for licentiousness, Molière for nonpayment of debts. *Tartuffe* was banned by Louis XIV for immorality until he changed his mind and the play became the most successful first run in the theater troupe's history.

The hyperactive network of gossip about his private life made Molière sick: the stress of it, on his health and his marriage—in addition to his having to make the troupe financially solvent while writing and directing the plays and performing their lead roles for months on end—weakened his lungs. Pulmonary disease killed him. He coughed to death in 1673 either on stage during a performance of *Le Malade imaginaire* or at home just across from the Théâtre Française at *40, rue de Richelieu* (now marked with a plaque). (The *Fontaine Molière* stands at the corner of *rue Molière*.)

The Church refused him a religious funeral and burial

because as an actor he was *un excommunicat*. His wife tried to get a priest from *Saint-Eustache* to come to their home as he lay dying: Molière wanted to confess his sins, his life as an actor, a confession needed for burial in sacred ground instead of in a garbage dump. The priest refused.

Molière's wife, Armande Béjart, asked Louis XIV directly to approve a Christian burial for her husband. The king ordered the pastor of *Saint-Eustache* to disobey Church law and obey Louis. The pastor obeyed but, fearing the archbishop of Paris, he covered up this transgression of ecclesiastical rules. He allowed Molière to be buried in the cemetery of Saint-Joseph, off rue Montmartre, at night, not as the excommunicated actor Molière but as Jean-Baptiste Poquelin, with no Mass. His funeral procession was followed by his wife, his troupe, his many torch-bearing friends. There were no eulogies, no street lights, no music.

In the words of Donald Frame, "Molière valued human nature and never liked tyrants." His body was later transferred to Père Lachaise.

Nearby

FORUM DES IMAGES: *Forum des Halles, 2, rue du Cinema. Métro: Châtelet-Les Halles. Two minutes from the southeast door of Saint-Eustache. The commerce at the new Les Halles is in movies, not veggies. Deep underground, you find a large open space with many computer tables, bookshelves filled with books about cinema and cinéastes, free and open to the public. Readers work in silence. Next door, in the same building, is **Forum des Images**, films about Paris.*

*Take the elevator up to **Médiathèque Musicale de Paris**. This is an extraordinary library, a large quiet room filled with CDs,* *sheet music, DVDs, vinyls that can be withdrawn. Many stock computers tell which branch library carries individual musicians, such as Satie, Poulenc, Patti Smith, et al. A few flights up are five movie theaters of various sizes where you can see films (the programs are posted downstairs near the cinema bookstore). The library is named for François Truffaut. There's a café, lounge, and restrooms nearby.*

BOUTIQUE-LIBRAIRIE DE LA COMÉDIE-FRANÇAISE: *2, rue de Richelieu. Hours: Mon–Sun, 1–7; closed Tues. An excellent selection of books on theater and French literature.*

BIBLIOTHÈQUE NATIONALE DE FRANCE, SITE RICHELIEU: *58, rue de Richelieu. Guided visits by prior arrangements: visites@bnf.fr. Opened in 1692. Salle Ovale: Henri Labrouste's wrought iron frame supporting a cluster of faience cupolas suspended over the main reading room. This is one of the most beautiful rooms in the world.*

RUE MOLIÈRE: *On the corner of this street, just north of Place André Malraux, is the Fontaine Molière, by Visconti (sculptor of the fountain in Place Saint-Sulpice), with a statue of Molière and marbles by Pradier.*

Related Reading

Donald Frame, *Molière*

Saint-Merri

SAINT-MERRI

LOCATION: 78, RUE SAINT MARTIN; 76, RUE DE LA VER-
  RERIE
HOURS: Mon–Fri, 2–6, 7 in winter; Sat, 3–7; Sun, 10–1;
  concerts: Sat and Sun, 4, 5:30
MÉTRO: Hôtel de Ville; Châtelet
WWW.SAINTMERRY.ORG

The Saturday and Sunday weekend concerts at *Saint-Merri* lift your spirits. Some Parisians wouldn't think of missing any of them. "The nave turns into a music space," writes Ann Morrison in *City Secrets: Paris*. (Check the website for the concert schedule: *www.accueilmusical.fr*.)

But late on weekday afternoons in winter, when you're the only person wandering around in the shadows, the church of *Saint-Merri,* huge, with parts of it always being restored and full of scaffolding and ladders, can feel haunted. The past feels alive but not quite friendly.

Saint Medericus (originally Abbé Medericus of the great abbey at Autun) came to Paris on a pilgrimage in the eighth century. He stayed and later died here. During the last Viking siege of Paris in 884, Medericus, nicknamed "Merri" by now, was declared patron saint of the Right Bank. Why? We don't know.

The church stands at the crossing of the old Roman road, *rue Saint-Martin,* running north and south, and the east-west crossing, the *rue de la Verrerie*. (Legend has it that Boccaccio [1313–1375], whose mother was French, was born in the area of this intersection.) Maybe the interior of the church feels so ancient because its environs remain ancient, the buildings and narrow alleys, the cobblestones; there are no cars in sight. Victor Hugo set parts of *Les Misérables* here, where anti-monarchist barricades were set up in the riots of 1832.

The modern does insert itself on the church's exterior northern flank: there's a large border occupied by a plaza—now, one of the liveliest squares in the city center—between the *Pompidou Centre* and the pool of the *Stravinsky Fountain* (1983), its waving mobile and dancing sculptures boldly colored, wowing tourists. It's dedicated to the Russian composer Igor Stravinsky (1882–1971), who lived in Paris on and off; he wrote the music for the ballets *Petrushka* (1911) and *The Rite of Spring* (1913), first performed in Paris.

On entering *Saint-Merri* through the western doorway, be sure to look at its amazing frieze of medieval sculpture, all recently restored. The bell tower above this west front shelters the oldest bell in Paris, cast in 1331. The bell still works.

A century later into the late Middle Ages, *Saint-Merri* was the home ground of *Jean Beaupere,* parish priest and a notoriously misogynist theologian who weighed in on the case against Joan of Arc. He was one of her first inquisitors. After her capture and during the trial, she had been accused of witchcraft: for one thing, she insisted on wearing men's clothing on and off the battlefield. The screed issued by *Beaupere,* which influenced the imposition of the death penalty by the Sorbonne luminaries—Joan was burned alive in Rouen in 1431—is chilling in its disgust for the young woman who trusted the voices of her conscience and would not back down as *Beaupere* badgered her and sneered during long days of interrogation. (After her murder, *Beaupere,* though some churchmen in Rouen were moved to tears, trashed Joan's memory: "She had had the wiles of a woman," he said.)

I prefer to enter *Saint-Merri* around the corner, through the entrance on *rue de la Verrierie, no. 76*. (Bulletin boards in the entrance lobby post information about the many concerts and community activities taking place at *Saint-Merri*.) Just inside the southern entrance you come face-to-face with a wooden sculpture of "The Dejected Man." He is also called "the Christ." He sits, his rigid long back flat against a stone pillar, narrow bodied and expressionless; stiff. He looks unloved, without desire, wrapped in an impenetrable sorrow. He is the quintessential rejected human being, alienated, alone, the kind of person religions exist to comfort. The image represents the mission of this church: it is dedicated to helping immigrants who live on the streets of Paris find housing, jobs, the required papers. *"Sans-Papiers, Mais Pas Sans Droits"* ("Without papers, but not without rights") is one of its mottoes.

(In 2020 in New York City, during the pandemic, the "Dejected Man" and hundreds of his brothers—["the homeless" of the Upper West Side]—were described as "subhuman" by West Siders who called for the services of "animal control" to clean up the valuable real estate of the neighborhood. See the *New York Times*, August 19, 2020, A5.)

Across from "The Dejected Man," above the altar on the church's south side, is a painting of the pilgrims of *Emmaus*. (*Abbé Pierre* was welcomed into the pulpit of *Saint-Merri* when he founded the *Emmaus* movement to rescue the homeless; he was looking for volunteers and publicity. See p. 55).

Moving into the main aisle, you turn to your right and there straight ahead is the heavily gilded *Glory* rising into the air over the main altar: it's a large burst of gold—signifying

La Madeleine

LA MADELEINE

LOCATION: **PLACE DE LA MADELEINE**
HOURS: 9:30–7
MÉTRO: Madeleine
WWW.EGLISE-LAMADELEINE.COM

The most beautiful approach to the *Madeleine (the church of Sainte-Marie-Madeleine)* starts in the *Place de la Concorde*; walk straight north (the *Seine* at your back), up the hill of *rue Royale,* where at the summit there rises, like a Greco-Roman temple, this monumental church. Turn around and stand facing downhill from the Corinthian colonnade: there, directly opposite, in the distance, stands the Obelisk and across the river the *Assemblée nationale,* the Corinthian façade of the French Chamber of Deputies matching that of *la Madeleine.* The counterbalancing of these two massive symbols of Church and State show a perfect symmetry: it signifies the balance of the two parts of the power structure of *la belle France.*

Directly beneath you, as you stand on the front steps of the church, is the spacious *Place de la Madeleine.* There has been a church in this *quartier*—known as the *Ville l'Éveque* since the bishop of Paris owned the land—since the sixth century; it became a temple dedicated to Saint Mary Magdalene in the thirteenth century. Several smaller churches were built and then razed as the city grew in size and population after the Revolution.

This massive church, which you're about to enter, was

begun in 1806 by order of Napoleon, who revised the design many times. He wanted a *Temple de la Gloire*, not so much a temple to God as a temple to the French army. The building was completed in 1845 when *la Madeleine* became "the society church of Paris."

It's not hard to imagine scenes from the **Place de la Madeleine**'s post-Revolution past. The construction sites; the cartouches; the mash of carriages, hearses; the elegant churchgoers: the top-hatted gentlemen bankers escorting wives and families; an assortment of philandering hypocrites out of Émile Zola's novel *Nana* transformed on Sunday mornings into proud parishioners with deep pockets, taking their Sunday pews in *la Madeleine,* bowing discreetly to one another up and down the long hyperdecorated nave.

Many society weddings and funerals began in the **Place**. Invited guests, power couples and their offspring, descending from carriages, made their way up the steps and across the colonnade as organ music swelled, accompanying them into the dark church.

Benita Eisler, in her engaging biography of Frédéric Chopin (1810–1849)—*Chopin's Funeral*—focuses her opening chapter on his great society funeral:

> *On a sparkling Paris morning, Tuesday, October 30, 1849, crowds poured into the square in front of the Church of the Madeleine. The occasion was the funeral of Frédéric Chopin, and for it, the entire façade of the great neoclassical temple had been draped in swags of black velvet.... Admission was by invitation only: Between three thousand and four thousand had received the black-bordered cards.... Hector Berlioz reported that "the whole of artistic and aristocratic Paris was there."*

Chopin had planned his funeral's program: he had adored Mozart in his lifetime (though Bach came first) and Haydn. He wanted Mozart's *Requiem* sung. When the archbishop of Paris reminded Chopin's friends that women were forbidden to sing in church, someone persuaded the archbishop to make an exception when it came to Chopin's funeral. The archbishop gave in, almost. He'd allow the women to sing only if they remained invisible. Their voices and bodies must be contained behind a black velvet curtain, thus muffling the women's voices and hiding their curves.

Outside the church, on a front door of *la Madeleine,* there is a bronze relief of a shamed woman hiding her face. The relief represents one of the Ten Commandments: *Thou shalt not commit adultery.*

The adulterous woman, who represents **Saint Mary Magdalene,** signifies the sinfulness, in particular the sin of lust, of womankind, the children of Eve. (The Magdalene's sister in sin, Saint Mary of Egypt, you'll remember, stands carved in all her naked hairy shame, down the hill in the church of **Saint-Germain l'Auxerrois.** See p. 129).

At the end of the Mass, after Chopin's funeral march had been played by the organist and the organ had played Chopin's favorite pieces, the Preludes in E minor and B minor, the mourners descended the front steps and then gathered outside in the *Place de la Madeleine.* Soon the women who had loved him and his Polish female relatives followed his *corbillard*—the hearse—pulled by black horses, out of the *Place* and then three miles east to *Père Lachaise.* The women, veiled and weeping, followed on foot.

The cultural legacy of *la Madeleine* comes laden with irony. For a church as cold as the interior of *la Madeleine*—despite the

colored marble and abundant gold leaf; the saucer domes lining
the ceiling (seen as shallow horizontal slices of a hemisphere);
the many conventional paintings and sculptures; the looming
Ionic columns; side chapels and the majestic high altar featuring
an ascendant Magdalene, swirlingly ecstatic—the two musical
geniuses most closely associated with this *temple de la gloire*—
Frédéric Chopin and *Gabriel Fauré* (1845–1924)—are loved for
the sensuality and voluptuousness of their music.

Fauré has now come into his own. Composer, pianist,
teacher, and director at the Paris Conservatoire, choirmaster
and organist at *la Madeleine,* his discography includes hundreds
of titles of piano music, orchestral and chamber works, songs.
The popular performance pieces, the *Pavane,* the *Dolly Suite,*
the *Canticle of Jean Racine* (written when he was nineteen)—
are loved worldwide. His *Requiem,* first performed in 1888 and
now performed more than any other of his works, is a unique
masterpiece of religious choral music. The *Requiem* includes the
haunting melody of the "*Pie Jesu*" and the final tender movement
of "*In Paradisium.*" It has been called "A Lullaby of Death."

Fauré's emphasis came from his own attitude to death and
the afterlife:

> *That's how I see death: as a joyful deliverance, an aspiration
> towards a happiness beyond the grave, rather than a painful
> experience. . . . / The Requiem / is as gentle as I am myself.*

His son Philippe said that the heart of the work for his
father was the phrase *"Quia pius est"* (For thou art merciful).
His pupil Nadia Boulanger said Fauré understood religion
more after the fashion of the tender passages in John's Gospel, following Saint Francis of Assisi, rather than the warn-
ings of Saint Bernard. His voice interposed itself between

heaven and man; usually peaceful, quiet and fervent, sometimes grave and sad, but never menacing or dramatic. "*He offered a homage to Beauty in which there was not only faith, but a discreet yet irresistible passion.*"

With his dark Arabian eyes and bronze complexion—he came from a family rooted in the Mediterranean French southwest since the thirteenth century—he was irresistible to women. He had the charm of a southerner; his deep courtesy and capacity for intimacy and humor influenced his many love affairs and the music they inspired. Paris at the end of the nineteenth century turned a blind eye to adultery, which was common in the world of the salons, though divorce made high society Paris uncomfortable. Fauré had a wife and two sons but he lived an active nightlife in the salons of the wealthy *arrondissements*, playing music, talking music, meeting old and new friends, falling in love.

Marcel Proust was a frequent salon guest. He loved Fauré's music and said he knew it well enough to write a three-hundred-page book about it. Fauré was sometimes the guest of honor at Proust's salon. The sensibilities of Proust and Fauré, according to one biographer, are similar, a balance between the intellectual and the sensual. Fauré, in the words of biographer Jessica Duchen, is central to the idea of "music as a premonition of the beyond," which is also central to the vision of Proust. Another biographer noted that Proust found in Fauré "the blend of sensuality and mysticism" that he expressed in his own work.

Fauré did not become organist and choirmaster of *la Madeleine* until many years after Chopin's funeral. In both roles he was able to pay the rent and buy food for his family as he oversaw the liturgies of *la Madeleine* and put up with the interference of the priest in charge. As teacher and then as director of the *Conservatoire*, he was an important influence on—and friend of—Maurice Ravel and Nadia Boulanger. Camille Saint Saëns, who had been his childhood teacher, was his lifelong friend and surrogate father.

When he was a little boy, the youngest of six children, before he moved away to music school in dark gloomy Paris at the age of nine, he played alone in the sun-drenched family garden not far from the Pyrenees. It was "filled with fragrant pines, cedars, magnolias, fruit trees and flowers," as Duchen describes it. The beauty of his childhood world left a lasting and deep impression on his developing consciousness.

> *His music has a sense of space, air, light, even fragrance, the opposite of the Paris music school and the dark oppressive church known as the Madeleine.*

When he died in 1924, his *Requiem* was performed at his state funeral in *la Madeleine*. Like Beethoven when he died, Fauré had been completely deaf for twenty years.

The memorial concert in *la Madeleine* on November 11, 2018, in commemoration of the Great War (1914–1918), playing to an almost full church, blasted Telemann's trumpets, Haydn and Mozart's horns and strings, jubilant, mournful, as the 1,697,800 French dead were recalled.

Nearby

LA CHAPELLE EXPIATOIRE: *The Expiatoire Chapel, Square Louis XVI, 29, rue Pasquier, the eighth arrondissement. **Métro: Saint-Augustine**. Open Thurs, Fri, Sat, 1–5. A chapel built to commemorate the ancien régime—Louis XVI and Marie Antoinette were buried here after their execution—on top of the old cemetery of **la Madeleine** with hundreds of corpses from the*

French Revolution. It is located halfway between **la Madeleine** *and the Gare Saint-Lazare. In 1814 when Louis XVIII took the throne, he moved the bodies of Louis XVI and Marie Antoinette from this Revolutionary Cemetery to the Basilica of Saint-Denis (see p. 190). The architecture of this chapel and the surrounding garden are well worth a visit.* **Chapelle-expiatoire-paris.fr.**

CHURCH OF SAINT-LOUIS D'ANTIN: *63, rue de Caumartin, a three-minute walk north off boulevard Haussmann.* **Métro: Havre-Caumartin on Saint-Lazare.** *Plain façade, dazzling and prayerful inside. Novelist Georges Bernanos (*The Diary of a Country Priest; Mouchette; Dialogue of the Carmelites*) was baptized here and grew up in the parish.* **L'Espace Bernanos, 4, rue du Havre** *(a block away), offers many parish activities and classes: Gregorian chant in La Salle* **Messiaen;** *the Hebrew Bible in La Salle* **Claudel;** *Bernanos's novels in La Salle* **Péguy.** *The funeral of* **Édouard Manet,** *who lived nearby, was held here. On a cold rainy night in December, a large vagrant man, during the Exposition of the Blessed Sacrament, was sprawled out on a rear row of seats, sleeping it off, snoring loudly, dead to the world. No one disturbed him. No one shot disapproving looks. One elderly woman stood up, crossed the middle aisle to cover him with her coat. No more snoring. "A church," said the priest to a judgmental woman in Bernanos's novel* The Diary of a Country Priest, *"is for everyone."*

Related Readings

Denis R. McNamara, *How to Read Churches: A Course in Ecclesiastical Architecture*

Jessica Duchen, *Gabriel Fauré*

Benita Eisler, *Chopin's Funeral*

Charles Koechlin, *Gabriel Fauré*

Sainte-Trinité

SAINTE-TRINITÉ

LOCATION: **PLACE ESTIENNE-D'ORVES**
HOURS: Will be posted after the restoration
MÉTRO: Haussmann; Saint-Lazare

The schedule of weekly evening concerts in la Trinité are posted on the rear left wall of the church as you face the main altar. There are also a few concerts on mid-weekdays.

Imagine you're walking in Paris just before noon on a warm blue-sky Saturday in June. The streets are almost deserted. You're looking for *la Trinité,* a church in the ninth *arrondissement*, east of the *Gare Saint-Lazare.* You come to a square hidden inside a grove of trees in full bloom, swarms of little birds twittering in and out of them; the birds fly explosively through a surround of three fountains, benches arranged on a curve, rhododendrons. Tall above the square, facing over *rue Saint-Lazare,* is an elegant church.

You've walked from *la Madeleine* and *Saint-Louis d'Antin* off *boulevard Haussmann.*

You choose a bench under a full noon sun for you and your tired feet. On a bench next to you some girls are chatting; a couple talks softly; some oldish men are wrapped in silence, one smoking. There're always a few people reading books or newspapers in Paris squares and parks. At our backs are the vibrations of light traffic from *rue Saint-Lazare.*

Without attitude, someone asks the smoker to stop smoking. He does. But then he takes off.

I stay sitting, just tasting the place. I can't force myself to stand up and climb the few steps to the church entrance. I am loving Paris, deliriously on this sunny Saturday, sitting here, watching, listening.

Place d'Estienne-d'Orves is named for the *Resistance* hero *Henri Honoré d'Estienne d'Orves* (1901–1941), murdered by the Nazis at Fort du Mount Valérien; there's a modest statue in his memory concealed by trees in the northwest corner of the *Place*. A church or chapel with a garden or a cemetery attached to it has a special charm in Paris: *Sainte-Clotilde. Notre-Dame. Saint-Germain l'Auxerrois. Saint-Ambroise. Saint-Germain de Charonne. Place Saint-Gervais. Picpus Cemetery*. And more.

The interior of *la Trinité* also has a distinctive charm. It's eclectic and cool and full of stillness. There are numerous side chapels and a modest main altar where on this particular Saturday there's a baptism in progress. A circle of grandparents, parents, godparents, aunts, uncles, cousins, and friends surround the font. No part of this altar or the church itself is triumphal. The balance of the designing architect's eye— *Théodore Ballu* (1817–1885)—has inspired a beautiful sanctuary. The celebrating priest is friendly to the family; the baby cries on and off. Two young boys—six-year-olds in matching blue blazers—scoot down the altar steps over to a side aisle where the confessionals stand at the edge of a small chapel: the kids hide inside, one in the box where the priest sits, the other in the penitent's. They're careful not to slam the doors of the confessional as they creep inside.

Wandering around *la Trinité,* I come upon a tall wooden statue in a side chapel at the head of the right aisle facing into the large nave. It's an image of *Sainte Geneviève*. Her statue and chapel have a spare dignity about them. There's also a plaque with information about the religious history of Paris and *Geneviève*'s role in it (see pp. 43-44). Maybe she's a legendary figure; maybe she's more fact than fiction. For the ages, no matter: artists depict her as a serious woman, a light in the core memory of Paris.

At the bottom of the right aisle, next to one of the front doors, is a wall plaque about the mystic and modernist composer *Olivier Messiaen* (1908–1992), chief organist at *la Trinité* for forty years. People came to *la Trinité* after the main Sunday Mass to hear *Messiaen* improvise and play for hours. (No tickets, no fee.) Next to the plaque is a glass cabinet containing *Messiaen* memorabilia, chronology, and selective discography. Most interesting to me is the background story of his composition of the religious ensemble *Quartet for the End of Time (Quatuor)*.

He wrote it in 1940 when he was a POW in a Nazi camp in Silesia. He had four instruments available to him: a clarinet, a piano that kept sticking, a broken violin that he mended, and a cello. It is "difficult" but life-affirming music. "I was never listened to," *Messiaen* said later in his journal, "with such attention and understanding." (Afterward, German guards would slip their "benign eccentric" prisoner sheets of paper and pencils.) The phrase "the end of time" in the title might be taken to refer to the hoped-for end of *Messiaen*'s incarceration but his reference is actually to the Angel of the Apocalypse, "who raises a hand to the heavens," saying: *"there shall be no more time."* His theme is the abolition of time itself, something infinitely mysterious to most philosophers of time, from Plato to Bergson.

Messiaen was also an educated ornithologist (he could

identify the sounds of seven hundred different birds); the songs of birds in his score destroy all symmetry. There is no similarity between his music and the Austro-German tradition of development, of working toward an end; the composer is contemplating the mystery of life to come. (Somewhere he wrote that birdsong was the first music heard in the Garden of Eden.) *Messiaen*'s most well-known composition is *Vingt regards [contemplations] sur l'Enfant Jésus,* twenty pieces performed more and more frequently by pianists in Carnegie Hall in New York City and in the halls of European cities. The glass cabinet also contains material about *Messiaen*'s friends and their music. Some were his students, Nadia Boulanger, Karlheinz Stockhausen, and Pierre Boulez; he was also influenced by Japanese and Hindu music.

Messiaen is a more and more popular modernist as contemporary audiences become more and more accepting of the mysteriousness of human consciousness and existence. His music expresses some of that.

Outside again on the church steps, I look down on the pool on the east side of the Square (to your left). What comes into my mind is the scene from François Truffaut's first movie, *The Four Hundred Blows,* where Antoine Doinel, his protagonist, washes himself here in the faint light of an early winter dawn. He's stayed out all night and needs to clean up before heading for school. Truffaut grew up on these streets of the ninth *arrondissement.* (See *33, rue Navarin, a few blocks east and a bit north.* See "Raising Hell in Pigalle," in *The Streets of Paris,* p. 206.) Truffaut later made these streets the set for many of his films.

One of the prettiest streetscapes in northern Paris is *rue Ballu,* named for the architect who built *la Trinité*. It's about a fifteen-minute walk north of *la Trinité* on *rue Blanche*; turn left at the corner into *rue Ballu*. Time is to be taken. Heading west on this quiet street, there you see *Villa Ballu* (nos. 1–7). Also no. 11, *rue Ballu*. You might walk this street west to east and back again many times. Visit the Villa. Visit SACD (Society of Authors and Dramatic Composers) at nos. 9–11. *www.sacd.fr.* Everything here is beautiful.

Théodore Ballu built other striking places in Paris: the church of *Saint-Ambroise* in the eleventh *arrondissement* (p. 218). *Sainte-Clotilde* on the Left Bank, its gorgeous evening concerts of sacred music as lovely as its architecture. He also rebuilt the *Hôtel de Ville* after it was set on fire by the Commune in 1871.

Nearby

LE DIT VIN: *68, rue Blanche. A charming small wine bar.*

CAFÉ DU MOGADOR: *Restaurant, brasserie. Directly across* rue Saint-Lazare *from the church of* la Trinité. *57, rue de la Chaussée d'Antin is the cross street. A warm and lively nineteenth-century café with good food in all seasons. Nice for Sunday brunch.*

Related Readings

Antoine de Baecque and Serge Toubiana, *Truffaut: A Biography*

Rebecca Rischlin, *For the End of Time: The Story of the Messiaen Quartet*

Stephen Schloesser, *Visions of Amen: The Early Life and Music of Olivier Messiaen*

The Grande Synagogue de la Victoire

THE GRANDE SYNAGOGUE
DE LA VICTOIRE

LOCATION: 44, RUE DE LA VICTOIRE

HOURS: Fri night, Shabbat service at 7:30 (dinner following, if reserved); Shabbat morning service, 9:30

MÉTRO: Notre-Dame-de-Lorette; Le Peletier

WWW.LAVICTOIRE.ORG

*"We would be delighted to welcome you to our syna-
gogue."*

The interior of *la Victoire* has the air of a profound serenity: it has truly the feeling of sanctuary. The beautiful
stained glass medallion and circular windows, of a calming
and mystical blue depicting the Twelve Tribes of Israel, border the long, high (eighty-seven-foot) rectangular ceiling. At
the head of the long rectangular middle aisle, the ark stands
high. The warmth of the synagogue's coloring, the blue glass
windows, the red velvet upholstery, the gold decoration,
and the gleaming white marble seem to celebrate this sacred
space.

Entering *la Victoire* as a stranger, making a first-time
visit, though I've walked past it many times, I was not ex-
pecting such a magnificent interior, nor its gracious and
warmhearted hospitality. (Institutional religion and its places
of worship can sometimes feel cold or exclusive.)

Outside on the sidewalk, as we foreign visitors and local Parisians waited on a Friday evening for Shabbat service to begin, for the usher to appear, unlock the gates, and lead us all inside, there was an openhearted bonhomie. I met a few Americans from the Upper West Side of New York City, a few Parisian families, some with kids in strollers. The usher, when he arrived, was full of jokes and curiosity: *Where are you from? New York*, I said. *The greatest city in the world!* said he, exclaiming with delight. *Come right in! Follow me!*

I had been warned that security would be strict at the **Grande Synagogue**. They'd check out everything in our bags and backpacks, including passports. Also: you had to be Jewish to enter a Paris synagogue.

None of that. Anyone from New York City, the usher's smile said, was a safe bet.

The men of the congregation sit in the center pews in the center aisle. (There are eighteen hundred seats in all.) At first there is no silence: congregants greet each other, hug, laugh. You can hear the pleasure in their greetings, the familiarity. These people are not strangers. Men and women move around, finding friends walking into the nave or arriving through the front doors.

The men of the congregation lead the chanting. The women's seats are positioned on raised platforms arranged along the two side aisles, to the right and left of the men, beneath the balconies on the second level. The separation of the sexes is common in many practices of the three Abrahamic religions—Judaism, Christianity, Islam; each came out of the Mediterranean world, each believes in one God. For many centuries, Christian women sat apart from men in Christian services. Women are still excluded from the ministry of the Catholic Church; the separation of the sexes also obtains in the Orthodox congregations of Judaism. At the Shabbat service in *la Victoire,* the cantor, who leads the chanting of the sacred texts, can be interpreted as a symbol of the one God who is worshipped as the Father of all. The chant, in a minor key, sometimes accompanied by a stringed instrument, recalls the tones and monotones of the ancient world and its music. That Judaism has evolved and survived over so many centuries, despite the persecutions it has endured, makes its performance every week in its own local synagogue a moving tribute to the strength of faith. For me, it was a privilege to be present.

The opulence of *la Victoire*—the brilliance of the chandeliers and candelabra, the lamplight gleaming on the marble—recalls the era when it was built: the Second Empire (1852–1870). The chief architect of Paris, Alfred-Philbert Aldrophe, built it as the largest synagogue in France, "the architectural jewel of the Jewish community in Paris," as Elaine Sciolino calls it in her book *The Only Street in Paris: Life on the Rue des Martyrs* (2016). *La Victoire* reflects the new wealth of the Jewish community in the late nineteenth-century city, its cultural richness and power. The Rothschilds, an international family of bankers throughout Europe, financed its construction. (*La Victoire* is also known as the Rothschild Synagogue.) Sciolino explains that *la Victoire* is located on this narrow off-the-beaten-track street because although the family of Emperor Napoleon III donated the land for the synagogue, his Spanish-born and rigid Catholic wife, Empress Eugénie, did not share her husband's affection for Jews. She disapproved of having an entrance to a synagogue between two nearby churches: *Sainte-Trinité* (see p. 163) and *Notre-Dame de Lorette.* "So the synagogue is oriented north, not east toward Jerusalem, as it should be," Sciolino writes.

From the beginning, *la Victoire* was the high society synagogue of Paris. The novelist and journalist Émile Zola (1840–1902) attended many weddings of Jewish friends here: he lived nearby in *rue Saint-Lazare* with his mistress and two children and in *rue de Bruxelles* with his wife. Whether he attended the wedding of Alfred and Lucie Dreyfus in 1890 at the *Grande Synagogue* is not known.

Zola was despised by conservative Parisians as morally corrupt; they were outraged by the animality of his novels' characters and plots, especially *Nana* (1880), in which wealthy Christian bankers go to Mass on Sunday mornings but exploit prostitutes and courtesans such as Nana on the days and nights before and after the sacred liturgy. (See *la Madeleine,* p. 155.)

Zola and Alfred Dreyfus are remembered in our time as moral heroes. They almost lost their lives for their commitment to justice. Their life stories, deeply woven together in the historical memory of Paris and *la Victoire,* reveal a labyrinth of institutional crime and punishment—Church and State the criminals—that remained the shame of the City of Light as the nineteenth century moved into the twentieth.

Alfred Dreyfus (1859–1935), a captain in the French Army, was arrested in 1894 on trumped-up charges of spying for Germany. Tried and convicted of treason, he was sentenced to life imprisonment on Devil's Island in 1895, one of the *Îles du Salut,* off the coast of French Guiana in South America. A Jew from a wealthy family, Dreyfus became the army's convenient scapegoat: it doctored evidence against him with the support of high-ranking military officers and Catholic clergy. Both the army and the Church had a centuries-long history of anti-Semitism. The wealth of the Jewish community aroused a murderous resentment in both institutions. France welcomed many Jewish refugees from the Russian pogroms of the 1880s, but the Parisian bourgeoisie resented how many Jews immigrated and how quickly they became rich.

The Dreyfus Affair dragged on for years, through a fetid mud of lies, sham trials, retrials, riots, and court-martials as the convicted Captain Dreyfus suffered in solitary confinement in a claustrophobic stone cell on a starvation diet, shackles on his legs, with only a view of the sky. In Paris, unknown to him, he had many supporters working to overturn the verdict and retry his case. His wife, Lucie, was his first and most loyal defender. (In her letters, she called him "my darling Fred.") Another was the Chief Rabbi of the *Grande Synagogue*, *Zadoc Kahn* (1839–1905), revered as a kind of prophet, an eminent scholar, an eloquent speaker, and a fearless advocate for social justice. Dreyfus's other most notable defender was *Émile Zola*, whose *"J'Accuse,"* his fiery defense of Dreyfus and an attack on the Church and the army, was published in a Paris newspaper. Zola exposed the criminality of the case against Dreyfus, an ecclesiastical–military conspiracy; then he was tried himself for libeling both Church and State, convicted, sentenced.

Eventually, there was a partial and bitter justice for Dreyfus (and Zola), but the riots of anti-Semitic mobs staged by the right-wing opposition scarred French history with an ugly legacy that has never disappeared.

In reaction to the role played by the Catholic Church in the Dreyfus Affair, a Republican government in December

1905 passed a "Law of Separation." "Catholicism," as Frederick Brown explains in *For the Soul of France*, no longer had any official status; emoluments and special considerations were outlawed. Secularism (*laïcité*) became the law of the land: Catholic schools and parish churches were closed, there was an exodus of religious orders, though the fight with the Church and anti-republicanism raged on.

The Dreyfus Affair showed its criminal legacy at the beginning of World War II when the French police played a role in the Holocaust, arresting and deporting seventy-five thousand Jews, who were French citizens, on the orders of the Nazi occupiers and the Vichy (French) government. The French police and the Gestapo made regular raids at *la Victoire* (and many other synagogues), arresting and deporting families and individual parishioners. (Their names appear in the entrance lobby of *la Victoire* and other Paris synagogues and the *Shoah Memorial*. See p. 201.)

The granddaughter of Alfred and Lucie Dreyfus, **Madeleine Dreyfus**, a *résistante,* was arrested and murdered at Auschwitz. **Lucie Dreyfus**, *née* Hadamard, married Captain Alfred Dreyfus at the *Grande Synagogue* in 1890, and survived her husband by ten years. During the Occupation she was hidden until the Liberation by Catholic nuns in the convent of the Good Shepherd at Valence in southeast France.

Nearby

PLACE DES VICTOIRES: *A short walk south from the church of* ***Notre-Dame des Victoires*** *(p. 135) to this elegant circular* **Place** *with an equestrian statue of Louis XIV. His horse is rearing; the "Sun King" sits high in the saddle. The* **Bourse,** *the Paris Stock Market, is nearby. The* **Place** *is also the setting of the movie*

Paris, Je t'aime (2006), *with Juliette Binoche—a collection of eighteen short films—by Japanese director Nobuhiro Suwa and others.*

RUE DES MARTYRS: *Métro:* **Saint-George** *north of* **la Victoire,** *between the church of* **Notre-Dame de Lorette** *and* **Place des Abbesses.** *A colorful walk uphill, passing good food shops, bistros, clothing stores, bars, cafés, and wine and cheese shops.*

Related Reading

Piers Paul Read, *The Dreyfus Affair*

Ruth Harris, *Dreyfus: Politics, Emotion, and the Scandal of the Century*

Frederick Brown, *For the Soul of France: Culture Wars in the Age of Dreyfus*

Elaine Sciolino, *The Only Street in Paris: Life on the Rue des Martyrs*

Notre-Dame d'Auvers-sur-Oise

VINCENT VAN GOGH'S MONTMARTRE
AND NOTRE-DAME D'AUVERS-SUR-OISE

LOCATION: 54, RUE LEPIC, MONTMARTRE

AUVERS-SUR-OISE: Train from *Gare du Nord* to
Auvers-sur-Oise (see *www.transilien.com/en*)

YOUTUBE VAN GOGH IN PARIS: MONTMARTRE (*www*
.youtube.com/watch?v=dyo4wkVtUvc).

Van Gogh: The Life, *the 2012 biography by Steven Naifeh
and Gregory White Smith—"magisterial," "captivat-
ing," "monumental," to quote a few critics—offers pilgrims and armchair travelers a compelling introduction to
van Gogh, especially the last chapters that depict his final
two and a half months in the village of Auvers-sur-Oise,
now a forty-five-minute train ride from Paris. The medieval church,* **Notre-Dame d'Auvers,** *inspired one of the
paintings he loved most.*

MÉTRO: to and from Gare du Nord. Check the above
website for times and changes of trains from **Gare du
Nord** to **Auvers-sur-Oise.**

V*incent van Gogh* (March 30, 1853–July 29, 1890) spent
much of his early life in Holland, where he was born
in Zundert (Brueghel had lived nearby) and first discovered
the beauty of nature. After he left home at sixteen, he tried
selling art prints; he tried evangelical religion—preaching to
the poor miners, to farmers (*The Potato Eaters*)—he studied
Latin, Greek, and Scripture in order to enter a Protestant

seminary. He failed at all of them. His father, a Calvinist minister, was disappointed in his peculiar oldest son: he had little sympathy for nonconformity. Like the parson, Vincent's entire family, especially his mother who did not like him, became increasingly unforgiving.

Vincent made a number of trips to Paris in those early years, where his younger brother Theo worked selling art, promoting young artists, wearing a suit, and earning a regular salary. He helped Vincent out with money, put him up in his apartment on *54, rue Lepic* in Montmartre (marked with a plaque and a ten-minute uphill walk from the *Abbesses Métro*) and encouraged his brother when in 1880 Vincent renounced organized religion and became a full-time artist. All their lives Vincent and Theo wrote letters to each other, extraordinary, heartbreaking, the best writing about art there is. Theo was his troubled brother's confidant.

Vincent had not a conventional bone in his body: he lived in his imagination, in another world. Theo understood, and loved him deeply. Theo's associates in Paris and the other artists Vincent met there thought he was a crazy man. No one except Theo ever saw that Vincent van Gogh was a visionary. In Paris, though Impressionism was on its way out in the 1880s, while living there Vincent discovered in it the use of brilliant color; he saw what he could do with light, with line; he discovered the power of Japanese prints in the lower Montmartre shop of *Père Tanguy* in *rue Clauzel* (still in operation at *no. 14; métro, Saint-Georges*). Van Gogh's brushstroke changed, partly influenced by pointillism. He went often to the Louvre; he adored the Rembrandts and the Delacroix—Delacroix, he saw, could express tenderness in the most violent colors. (Van Gogh kept prints on his wall of

Delacroix's *Pietà* and *Christ sur le lac de Genesareth*.) Though he had given up organized religion, van Gogh never gave up Jesus. Or Nature. He looked on Nature as a sacred sanctuary from which to draw solace or gather strength.

As Vincent worked in Paris, trudging up and down the twisty, hilly streets of Montmartre and Clichy; carrying his easel, canvases, stretchers, paints, and brushes; working *en plein air*; feeling the nasty blasts of passersby's ridicule; selling nothing; drinking in cafés; and spending Theo's money, he felt more and more alien in the City of Light.

But his art changed. He turned away from the dull stone coloring of northern painting—his father's church (*The Old Church Tower at Nuenen*)—as he began to understand what the radiance of Impressionism could communicate, that the experiment of working in and under the sun was a way to know God. *God is in everything, except in the church and my bloody family*. He believed now in the gospel of color.

But after one disappointment after another, getting nowhere, he left Paris and moved south to Arles in Provence. He invited Paul Gauguin to join him.

That story is well-known: the two artists sharing the Yellow House, with Gauguin coming to despise Vincent and his strange behavior; their fights; and Vincent, in a rage, slicing off part of his own ear and delivering it into the hands of a favorite prostitute.

Gauguin ran. Back to Paris. Theo arrived to deliver his unhinged brother to an asylum near **Saint-Rémy**. More than a year later, Vincent was pronounced cured and he returned to Paris and Theo. His rages were never diagnosed. Epilepsy? Schizophrenia? Syphilis? Paint poisoning? (When manic, Vincent ate his paints right out of the tubes.) In the twentieth century, his dark fits—the periods of mania followed by deep depressions—might have been called bipolar disorder.

By this time, Theo was married, his wife and baby son—"Vincent"—sharing his apartment.

After three days in Paris, Vincent caught the northbound train to *Auvers-sur-Oise,* a picturesque country village overlooking the river Oise, less than twenty miles from Paris, where many painters had worked (Corot, Daumier, Pissarro, Renoir, Monet, Daubigny, and Cézanne). Theo had praised the riverbank town, thought Vincent should try it out.

He took the train at the *Gare du Nord*. (*"All the noise in Paris is not for me,"* Vincent told Theo.)

After a full day in *Auvers-sur-Oise,* following in van Gogh's footsteps, you feel closer to him than you ever do in Paris. For one thing, the streets of Paris are now clogged with cars, while the narrow country roads of *Auvers-sur-Oise* are as van Gogh knew them. You can see and breathe the beauty of nature. He called it an Eden. The golden fields, the plateau and the blackbirds flying high above, the cypresses, the view of the river Oise from the high road, the church. (There's not one church in Paris that is associated with van Gogh.) He admired the simplicity and strong lines of the old thatched farmhouses, their lovely front flower gardens. They're still there, along the roads winding west toward the house and garden of Dr. Gachet, whose help Theo had suggested his brother seek. Gachet had helped other artists.

As you leave the train, walk straight across the main road of **Auvers-sur-Oise** *to the* **office of tourism,** *with a bookshop, annotated maps (Office de Tourisme d'Auvers-sur-Oise; Touristic Map:* **Auvers-sur-Oise:** *Village d'Artistes), prints, and postcards; it's in a small Parc van Gogh (with restrooms and a statue* *of van Gogh by Ossip Zadkine). Return to the main road,* **rue du Général de Gaulle**, *bear right, and head west. You'll pass the mairie—the* **"town hall"**—*on your left, the subject of one of van Gogh's saddest paintings; across from it the* **Auberge Ravoux,** *(now the* **Maison van Gogh**, *the dining room open, with reservations), in van Gogh's time a cheap inn where he stayed for seventy days. Continue walking west on this country road, bearing left into* **rue Docteur Gachet**. *In another half-hour's walk,* **Maison du docteur Gachet** *(no. 78) appears on your right. In spring and summer Gachet's gorgeous flower gardens and trees appear on your right. The gardens, in van Gogh's time filled with fowl and the house with cats and dogs, are open to the public.*

Dr. Gachet, recommended to Theo by Pissarro, "gives the impression of being a man of understanding," Theo wrote to his brother.

Dr. Gachet has been blamed and praised for his treatment of van Gogh. His thesis in medical school—"A Study of Melancholy"—marked his lifelong interest in different forms of alienation and nervous diseases in artists. He practiced electrotherapy, allopathy, and homeopathy. Every Sunday he invited van Gogh to dinner with his grown children. Van Gogh painted Gachet's daughter, Marguerite, playing the piano. Gachet visited Vincent at the *Auberge Ravoux*. His attentions did little to heal the loneliness and guilt that tortured Vincent the longer he stayed in *Auvers-sur-Oise,* painting frantically and prolifically (seventy-eight masterpieces), pursued by the terror that his "dark fits" would return and he'd wind up confined in yet another asylum. His brother Theo did not visit with the baby. Vincent had no friends. Teen-aged boys chased him all over town, shouting *"fou"* (crazy). At night he went alone into the fields and, as he had in Arles and Saint-Rémy, painted the stars. He had always sensed a sacred presence in the night sky (*Starry Night Over the Rhône* and *Starry Night in St. Rémy*). As he wrote to Theo in 1888: "*I have an immense need for—shall I dare say the word— religion—so I go outside at night to paint the stars.*"

At the other end of town from Dr. Gachet's house, he found the Gothic church, **Notre-Dame d'Auvers,** up a hill (behind **Parc van Gogh**), overlooking the town, where it had stood since 1170. Van Gogh loved the Romanesque tower and buttressed apse, a sort of higgledy-piggledy building as you walk toward it. In his painting *The Church at Auvers* (now in the **Musée d'Orsay** in Paris), he made the whole building glow with bright colors, quite intentionally the opposite of the gray stone Protestant church his father ruled in Holland. The grass around Vincent's **Auvers** church, he wrote, shines in violet, beneath the "simple, deep, pure cobalt" sky. A slab of bright orange roof jars the rambling old building to life; a "pink flow of sunshine" embraces it.

The squat yet Gothic church you see today is the same one that Vincent loved, but the thick layers of bright colored paints he had covered its exterior with have been washed away. Inside, there's no unusual decoration (except for a traditional statue of Joan of Arc). If you visit **Auvers-sur-Oise** on a hot summer day, after walking its main streets and climbing its hilly side roads, the interior of the church at the end of your rambles is deliciously cool, like an ancient *frigdarium*.

Five minutes up the hill behind the church, along **Avenue du Cimetière,** Vincent and Theo are buried side by side beneath rectangles of stone leaning against the rear wall of the cemetery. From the graveyard you can look down on the Oise valley and the wheat fields above *Auvers-sur-Oise,* the river town that Vincent had loved at first—*"I'm almost too calm,"* he wrote when he found himself free of anxiety. Later it held the same dread as every other place he'd tried to live in since he'd left the Dutch hearth and home that did not want him there.

Vincent van Gogh's death remains a mystery. In 1890, when he died, on July 29, he entered history as a suicide. That was the story told to an interviewer by thirteen-year-old Adeline Ravoux, the daughter of the innkeeper who overheard her mother repeating rumors to guests at the inn. The *fou* painter had shot himself, said M. Ravoux, repeating the gossip she'd overheard.

But no one could find the gun.

The story told by the biographers Steven Naifeh and Gregory White Smith is more complex and convincing: Vincent van Gogh, they claimed, was a murder victim, deliberately shot by the teenage boy(s) who had tormented him since he'd arrived from Paris in May. After the shooting— perhaps accidental—the boys ran away, stayed away; the gun, which belonged to their father, was never found. Neither was Vincent's painting kit and easel that he carried with him everywhere. Vincent had confessed to suicide while dying in order to save the boys from a murder charge. He died a martyr. He was buried without a funeral from the church he had made immortal: as a suicide he had died in the state of mortal sin; church dogma would allow no prayers, no eulogies, no blessing.

Like Mozart, van Gogh had often calmed himself with the thought of death, the serenity of it, the eternal peace of paradise. But in the words of his biographers, mostly he inveighed against suicide, called it *"wicked"* and *"terrible"*—an act of *"moral cowardice"—"a crime against the beauty of life and the nobility of art."*

Nearby

SOUS LE PORCHE: **Place de la Mairie, Auvers-sur-Oise.** *A picturesque and friendly restaurant, good food. Friendly staff. Crowded weekends: reserve.*

L'AUBERGE RAVOUX: **52–56, rue du Général de Gaulle, Auvers-sur-Oise.** *Nicely restored since van Gogh lodged here and died in 1890. Opposite the Place de la Mairie, painted by van Gogh. Reserve.*

ÉGLISE NOTRE-DAME D'AUVERS: *Annual Festival d'Auvers-sur-Oise. In 2018 the program included the Orchestre de Chambre Nouvelle Europe. Tel: 01 30 36 77 77. festival-auvers.com. The festivals continue. The online photo galleries are lovely.*

Related Reading

Debora Silverman, *Van Gogh and Gauguin: The Search for Sacred Art*

Sue Roe, *In Montmartre: Picasso, Matisse and Modernism in Paris, 1900–1910*

Steven Naifeh and Gregory White Smith, *Van Gogh: The Life*

Jean-Jacques Lévêque, *Vincent van Gogh: The Path of Light*

The Basilica of Saint-Denis

THE BASILICA OF SAINT-DENIS

LOCATION: 1, RUE DE LA LÉGION D'HONNEUR

HOURS: Open: every day except Jan 1, May 1, Dec 25, and during certain services; April–Sept, 10–6:15; Sun, 12–6:15; Oct–March, 10–5; Sun, 12–5:15

MÉTRO: line 13 from La Fourche to Basilique de Saint-Denis

BASILIQUE-SAINT-DENIS@MONUMENTS-NATIONAUX.FR, WWW. SAINT-DENIS.CULTURE.FR/

*T*he Basilica of Saint-Denis—originally *"the Abbey Church of Saint-Denis"*—shows in sunlight an exterior façade of gleaming white stone, sandblasted and scrubbed not so long ago of its centuries of gray-brown grime. The statuary of its three huge doorways shows one lineup after another of sculpted saints' heads, prophets, kings, queens, and a few *synagogas* (headless or blind stone women wedged between carved ecclesiastical figures: these women, in the mind of the anonymous sculptor, see nothing, understand nothing, because they represent Jews who do not accept the Christianity that *Saint-Denis* celebrates. *Synagogas* also decorate other cathedral façades in Paris and throughout Europe. See Nina Rowe's *The Jew, The Cathedral and the Medieval City: Synagoga and Ecclesia in the Thirteenth Century*).

When you exit the métro, it's easy to follow the curve of the main street around the markets, bearing left, until you come into the wide, deep plaza fronting this basilica, cathedral, church, monastery, abbey (Saint-Denis has had multiple identities) and

187

the monumental doors that admit you to this sacred space, "one of the miracles of medieval architecture."

Inside, you realize at first glance that this magnificent Gothic church is well worth the métro ride of about forty minutes from Paris. The majesty of *Saint-Denis,* a building of such long history and beauty—you know at once that *Saint-Denis* requires time if you want to feel its presence. Few tourists get in your way.

It stands over the cemetery where, according to legend, Denis, the first bishop of Paris, sent by the pope to evangelize the Gauls of Lutetia, was buried following his murder in c. 258. The same legend has Denis carrying his severed head six kilometers up the hill of Montmartre (*mons martyrium*) after he was beheaded by the Romans in *rue Yvonne le Tac* near the *Temple of Mercury,* just east of *Place des Abbesses (and the Abbesses métro)*. Denis, the *cephalophoric,* the word for a martyr who carries his/her decapitated head to a resting place, was the first person to be buried here in what has been known as the Royal Necropolis since the third century. (There were forty-two kings buried here before they were dug up and dumped in 1789.)

The Abbey Church of Saint-Denis has, in the course of eighteen centuries, known many transformations: from "the Abbey of Saint Denis" founded by Saint Geneviève (c. 475); as a site of pilgrimage; as a Benedictine monastery said to be founded by *Abbé Suger*; as several churches of various sizes in honor of different kings and queens; as an abbey that Napoleon made into a basilica; in 1966 *Saint-Denis* became a cathedral.

Every student of medieval art and architecture knows the name "*Suger*" (c. 1080–1151) (pronounced *Soo-jay*). A powerful Benedictine monk and adviser to kings, as well as the guardian of the real estate while the kings were off on their

Crusades, he turned the **Saint-Denis Abbey** into the Gothic cathedral you are now observing.

To quote Diarmaid MacCulloch in *Christianity: The First Three Thousand Years*:

> *Nothing could be further from the Dark Ages than a Gothic cathedral: it is suffused with light, which is designed to speak of the light of Christian truth to all who enter it. Abbot Suger . . . one of the pioneering patrons of this new style, . . . had been seized by enthusiasm for the writings of Pseudo-Dionysius, mistaking that Eastern mystic for the martyred Saint Denis, patron of his own abbey, his corpse lying beneath it.*

The Syrian mystic Denis—and **Suger**—associated the quality of physical light with the experience of spiritual enlightenment *or with God himself.*

Suger's narthex, crypt, the buttresses, and the apse survive him today. The twelve lovely apse chapels of the ambulatory, their stained glass windows of unusual colors, show the "cycle of the Incarnation"; and in the chapel of the Virgin, they show the life of Mary, the mother of Jesus. All these were his inspiration. The ribbed vaulting of this church, each new flourish a component of the new Gothic art, establishes **Saint-Denis** as the birthplace of Gothic architecture. Look up at the extraordinary ceiling. At the light flooding the nave.

Suger's greatest achievement is, in my view, his use of glass and height to create the sense of a living light filling the nave and washing over the altar at the head of it. *God appeared and God is Light.* That was the heart of **Suger**'s theology.

As historian Alistair Horne writes in *La Belle France*, **Suger**'s delight in the sensuous world of light and color and design reveals a joie de vivre that inspired his talents as architect, engineer, and aesthete as well as the mysticism of the twelfth-century French Renaissance. He was also practical: a beautiful church that told stories in its embellishments would appeal to the common (illiterate) churchgoers. The stories of the Scriptures—the heart and soul of Christianity much more than the centuries of dogmatic theology—could be told through the medium of pictures and stories carved in stone.

Literary critic James Wood remembers his youth as a cathedral chorister in another medieval cathedral in England:

> *I spent long hours inside this magnificent building . . . and grew to love its gray silence, its massive, calm nave, the weight of centuries of devotion. Sometimes I could almost feel the presence of the faithful stonemasons . . .*

This is also a good description of **Saint-Denis** today.

For nine euros, you can visit the crypt below the church. The carved figures of recumbent kings and queens, the master with his curly hair, the mistress with her capped head and invisible hair, lie side by side atop their marble tombs or sarcophagi. Next to the section of the crypt filled with black onyx coffins and various tombs of the Bourbon dead (Louis XVI and Marie Antoinette), there is displayed inside a glass vessel hanging on a wall the petrified heart of their child, the uncrowned dauphin, Louis XVII, who is said to have died a few years after his parents.

The most haunting character whose story lives on in the stones of **Saint-Denis** is **Jeanne d'Arc,** or **Saint Joan of Arc** (1412–1431), or "**la Pucelle**"—"the maid," "the virgin," as she identified herself. There is no sign of her here today except for an inscribed plaque affixed in the wall to your right as you enter the basilica. On it are carved the brief details of her connection with the royal church.

As the world knows, she was the girl warrior who, urged by her heavenly "voices" and visions, enlisted in the Hundred Years' War (1337–1453) between France and England, to drive the English out of France and to support the coronation of the French dauphin as Charles VII.

At the head of her French troops, high on her horse, holding her standard and sword, wearing male armor, she won several military battles against the English (Orléans, for one, and in the Loire Valley the towns of Meung-sur-Loire, Jargeau, Beaugency, and Patay). Thanks to her, Charles was crowned at Reims in 1429. Once he wore the crown, the pusillanimous Charles VII began to trust her, for a time ignoring his advisors' voices: the nobles and soldiers of the French court and the clergy who insisted that this teenaged "slut" on a horse, armed, dressed like a man, was in fact a witch and a heretic.

As Joan and her army began to lose more battles than they won and Charles failed to provide Joan with fresh horses, cash, and gunpowder, the prize she craved eluded her. She and the French soldiers who remained loyal to her wanted to crash the defensive walls around Paris and deliver their capital from English occupation. Paris was about three miles south of where she and her troops were camped up at *La Chapelle* near the *Abbey of Saint-Denis.* King Charles opposed their plan. But eventually and reluctantly he gave her more troops and weapons for an attack on the gates of Paris. He ordered it to take place on Thursday, September 8, the feast of the Nativity of the Virgin. Joan left the camp at *La Chapelle* near *Saint-Denis* (a church remains in that area—*Saint-*

Denys de la Chapelle [1204])—for the three- to four-mile push south to the *Porte Saint-Honoré* in the walls that surrounded the center of Paris and protected the occupying English within. (You can see high on the wall of *Nos. 161–163, rue Saint-Honoré* a commemorative plaque in honor of Joan the Maid's assault on Paris and the place where she was wounded. That spot marks the beginning of her end.)

After a ten-hour battle, Joan, wounded, was ordered by the king to retreat and meet him at the *Abbey of Saint-Denis*.

At *Saint-Denis* she left her armor and her sword in the Lady Chapel, not in thanksgiving for a military victory or for surviving a recent war wound but, as biographer Donald Spoto puts it, "as a sign by which a soldier acknowledges that the battles are over, the race run." Or, in the words of historian Helen Castor, Joan's gift of her armor and sword to the Virgin was "an inscrutable acknowledgment of a task unfinished."

The king showed up, with new plans, new orders; Joan followed him, leaving *Saint-Denis* behind. Months later, at the battle of Compiègne, she was wounded again, but this time she was captured—ripped from her saddle, imprisoned, tortured, poisoned—a prize spoil of war. Eventually, after many twists, lies, and betrayals between the armies of France and England and the theologians and ecclesiastical judges of the University of Paris, she was convicted of heresy and burned alive in the Old Marketplace of Rouen in 1431. She was nineteen years old.

Noting the labyrinth of lies told by the churchmen, the rigged trial controlled by the English—fraudulent, corrupt, deceitful, slanderous, and malicious as the judges found it later—the resulting guilty verdict was overturned by ecclesiastical judges in 1456. They ordered a cross erected in the

Old Market square of Rouen to preserve Joan's memory forever.

She was declared a saint of the Church on May 16, 1920. Her feast day is May 30, the day she was murdered.

Her sword is said to remain in the archives of the *Basilica of Saint-Denis.*

At the end of the Hundred Years' War, the English were bankrupt and the French controlled every city in France except Calais.

During the French Revolution—in particular the *September Massacres* (see p. 78)—as part of the program of "dechristianization," *Saint-Denis* was ransacked, the figures of the statuary on the façade beheaded like the monks who lived inside the monastery. During the Reign of Terror (1793–1794), it is estimated that twenty to forty thousand members of the clergy were murdered and thirty thousand were forced to emigrate. Few of France's forty thousand churches remained open. Paris reeked of blood, severed heads, and body parts.

But *Jeanne d'Arc* has never disappeared: she remains grounded forever in the memory of Paris, whether sacred, secular, right-wing, left-wing, Socialist, Nationalist, Catholic, Protestant, or a combination of all these identities. She is honored as the national hero of France, the image of female heroism. The statues of her that stand throughout Paris (and many other cities) feature the holy warrior soldier, Republican and Napoleonic symbol for her opposition to the English and for all those who would protect France from foreign domination.

In World War II Charles de Gaulle used her standard, the Cross of Lorraine, as the symbol of Free France.

Artists have long made her the center of their most brilliant works: filmmakers Carl Dreyer, Robert Bresson, Jacques Rivette, and recently Bruno Dumont in his extraordinary (and prize-winning) heavy metal rock operas, *Jeanette: The Childhood of Joan of Arc* (*L'enfance de Jeanne d'Arc*, 2017) and *Joan of Arc* (*Jeanne*, 2019)—"*tender and lyrical*" to quote one critic—based on the poet Charles Péguy's play *The Mystery of the Charity of Jeanne d'Arc*. Biographies and novels run to the thousands. Mark Twain, an "agnostic misanthrope," to quote Donald Spoto, considered his novel about Joan, *Personal Recollections of Joan of Arc*, his best work. He called her "the most magnificent virtuous, thoroughly admirable person in the history of the world."

Nearby

LE KHÉDIVE: *A friendly café across the plaza fronting* **Saint-Denis**. *Visitors to the basilica and local people rest content and are well served in this local establishment.*

LE BASILIC: *Another good café, next to* **Khédive**. *Excellent* boeuf.

THE MARKETS OF SAINT-DENIS: *Just off the plaza. Large, sometimes crowded. There is nothing that is not sold here, shoes, CDs, clothing, household goods. A terrific produce market on Tues, Fri, and Sun mornings.*

STADE DE FRANCE: **métro 13 to Saint-Denis-Porte de Paris. Stadefrance.com. Closed Mon.** *A fantastic sports complex and concert venue, seating over eighty thousand. There's also a permanent exhibition covering all aspects of sport and entertainment. Several good restaurants within the Stade, plus snacks, crepes, halal, some with no service during events.*

Related Reading

Marina Warner, *Joan of Arc: The Image of Female Heroism*

Donald Spoto, *Joan: The Mysterious Life of the Heretic Who Became a Saint*

Nina Rowe, *The Jew, the Cathedral and the Medieval City: Synagoga and Ecclesia in the Thirteenth Century*

Charles Péguy, *The Mystery of the Charity of Jeanne d'Arc*

Saint-Gervais & Saint-Protais

The Marais

SAINT-GERVAIS & SAINT-PROTAIS

LOCATION: **PLACE SAINT-GERVAIS**
HOURS: Mon–Sun, 5:30–9; sung liturgy, Fri nights, 6. If
the front door is locked, enter from around the back
on *rue des Barres*
MÉTRO: Hôtel de Ville

P*lace Saint-Gervais* is a gracious hideaway, especially if
you need a break after walking the city from, say, the
Bois de Boulogne in the west toward Bois de Vincennes in
the east. The *Place* is ideal. You can sit on the front steps of
the church and watch life going by, fast, slow, loud: kids on
bikes; teenagers lounging on sidewalks; the murmur of conversation from pairs of women, couples, people getting off
and on the local bus; solitaries just dreaming away the afternoon. Sometimes there's not a soul in sight. Just the hulking
Hôtel de Ville across *rue de Lobau,* directly in front of you.
The *Seine* is nearby; this whole western stretch along the
Right Bank was once one of the busiest ports in Paris, a hub
of the *southern Marais.*

The church of *Saint-Gervais & Saint-Protais,* stately, an
architectural gem (named after two brothers from Milan who
were martyred by Nero), was, according to Italian sculptor
and artist Gian Lorenzo Bernini (1598–1680), the most perfect building he saw in seventeenth-century Paris. The façade features three columns of the three orders: Doric on the
ground floor; Ionic on the second (statues of the two martyrs
are tucked inside niches on the second level); Corinthian on

the third. This church, *Flamboyant Gothic* like **Saint-Séverin** (see p. 33), was begun in 1494, completed in 1578, though the parish goes back to the sixth century. Voltaire, who once rented nearby, could hardly contain his enthusiasm: *"C'est le plus beau morceau d'architecture qu'il y ait en France!"* ("This is the most beautiful piece of architecture there is in France!")

Another lovely sight on the **Place,** as lovely as any architecture, is the famous elm tree in the middle. As art historians tell it, all local streets once converged on this spot; it was under the elm that justice was administered, a story similar to the one about King/Saint Louis IX (see p. 26) administering justice to his subjects under the oak tree out in the **Bois de Vincennes.** Duels were fought here, too, all manner of scores settled.

So the **Place** and the façade of **Saint-Gervais & Saint-Protais** in the **southern Marais** are justly celebrated. But equally as beautiful, if not more, is the narrow cobblestone street behind the church—**rue des Barres** (thirteenth century) that leads up a slight hill to the church's rear entrance (which you can approach either from the north—**rue François Miron**—or the south side—**Quai de l'Hôtel de Ville.**)

As you ascend the slight hill of **rue des Barres** with the **Seine** at your back, you look up and see the magnificent south flank of the church. You pass some arcades that resemble an old cloister. Most dramatic is the roof of **Saint-Gervais & Saint-Protais,** so high and steep over the sacristy and the apse of the church. The old bell tower is visible, too, and several slanting gables. You pass a small garden on your left, full with healthy plantings, and, in season, outdoor tables and chairs, a café *en plein air.* Continuing up the hill, you see the delineations of the church's medieval sacristy and apse. A few small shops line the right side of the road (one with a good selection of religious objects) as well as outdoor seating for the pretty restaurant ***Chez Julien***. Once at the end of ***rue des Barres,*** turn around and look down over the gentle hill at the river. Across the ***Seine*** you see a stunning line of willow trees and *hôtels particuliers* on ***Île Saint-Louis's Quai d'Anjou***, where Daumier had his studio.

Entering ***Saint-Gervais & Saint-Protais*** through the rear door, you notice immediately the change in the light: outside there's sun (well, not always); inside you walk from shadow to shadow, as if caught in a perpetual late winter afternoon. But the ***Stalles Misericordes*** (***Stalles du choeur***), or choir stalls, are superb (with a pocket flashlight you can see the details or follow the story told by medieval woodcarvers). Toward the rear of the church, on the south side, there is the Commemorative Chapel, or the Chapel of the Victims, commemorating the bombing of ***Saint-Gervais & Saint-Protais*** by the Germans in World War I, on Good Friday, March 29, 1918; and a commemorative visual in memory of the victims of the Dresden bombing of February 13, 1945. (There is a booklet on sale in the rear of the church, "L'Église Saint-Gervais," with incredible photos of the wreckage piled high in the aisles of ***Saint-Gervais & Saint-Protais*** on that Good Friday.)

For music lovers, this church is known as "Couperin's Church." The "Couperin organ" was played by seven members of that family from 1653 to 1830. François Couperin, the master of the Baroque organ and harpsichord, a child prodigy who played it the longest (1685–1733), was the most prestigious musician in the family. ("The great French keyboard master," he is called.) His two Masses for the organ are still played. On November 10, 2018, Couperin's music was played at an anniversary concert in honor of the centenary of

World War I. Though the rain poured down, there was not an empty seat in "Couperin's Church."

(Two young French musicians, Thomas Dunford and Jean Rondeau, who play lute and harpsichord, recently collaborated on "Barricades," a collection of French Baroque music by Couperin, Charpentier, Rameau, and others, to extremely enthusiastic reviews. The music is *alive,* sounding the bold joy of the Baroque French sprezzatura.)

For music lovers devoted to liturgical music, there is, in the church of *Saint-Gervais & Saint-Protais,* on Friday nights at six, sung Evening Prayer (Vespers) followed by a sung Mass: the choirs consist of members of the parish's monastic communities, about a hundred monks and nuns of some twenty different nationalities comprising the *Communion of Jerusalem.* As urban monks and nuns, wearing white habits, they bear the name *Jerusalem* because Jerusalem is the patron of all cities. Their mission is to live and pray in the heart of the city. They rent their housing, hold part-time jobs, and have no walled cloister; there are places on the grounds of *Saint-Gervais & Saint-Protais* available for prayer and silence and living solo. Their Friday night liturgies are welcoming, full of spirit and good cheer. Parisians crowd the place, sometimes join in the singing, and at the kiss of peace there is much hilarity and bonhomie.

Nearby

PLACE DE GRÈVE: *On the west side of the **Hôtel de Ville** is the large square or strand or **grève** where ships anchored since the eleventh century. It was also the location for barbarous public executions, especially of Protestants, heretics, revolutionaries, and* criminals. *The medieval poet and **Beguine, Marguerite Porete,** was imprisoned for a year and then burned at the stake here in 1310 for refusing to speak to her inquisitor. She was the first French Christian mystic to be murdered for heresy and for her heretical book,* The Mirror of Simple Souls *(see* Wise Women, *ed. Susan Cahill). Now this space functions as an ice rink in winter, outdoor movies on summer nights, and an extension to Paris Plage, a stretch of riverbank with swimming in summer.*

CAFÉ-RESTAURANT LOUIS PHILIPPE: *A homey place, with delicious home-cooked food. A friendly clientele and staff, with panoramic views of the **Seine** and **Île Saint-Louis.***

LE PIÉTON DE PARIS: *An excellent French bookshop, with classic French literature. Two minutes east of **Saint-Gervais** at 58, **rue de l'Hôtel de Ville,** near the corner.*

SHOAH MEMORIAL: *(www.memorialdelashoah.org) A five-minute walk east from Saint-Gervais at 17, **rue Geoffroy l'Asnier. Open Sun–Fri, 10–6; Thurs, 10–10; closed Sat.** The modern building (1956) combines the memorial to an unknown Jewish martyr, archives, a photo library, library, museum, and an excellent bookshop. I found my copy of Hélène Berr's* Journal, *a memoir of the Holocaust in Paris, here. The names of seventy-six thousand Jews deported from France are engraved on the Wall of Names in the forecourt. The Wall of the Righteous bears the names of those who helped Jews find safety.*

CHURCH OF SAINT-PAUL SAINT-LOUIS (OR THE GRANDS JESUITES): *9, **rue Saint-Antoine, south side. Métro: Saint-Paul. Hours: Sun–Mon, 8–8.** Built by Louis XIII, 1627–41, restored in the nineteenth century, its ornate florid style inspired by the mother church in Rome, the Gesú. It's a good example of*

French Jesuit architecture, to quote The Blue Guide. *The paint-ing* Christ in the Garden of Olives *by Delacroix is in the north transept. It was the parish church of* **Madame de Sévigné.**

Related Reading

Marguerite Porete, *The Mirror of Simple Souls,* in Classics of Western Spirituality and in *Wise Women,* ed. Susan Cahill

Jane Hirshfield, ed., *Women in Praise of the Sacred: 43 Centuries of Spiritual Poetry by Women*

Joan DeJean, *How Paris Became Paris: The Invention of the Modern City*

Synagogue de Nazareth

SYNAGOGUE DE NAZARETH

LOCATION: 15, RUE NOTRE-DAME DE NAZARETH
HOURS: Shabbat, Sat, 10. Tel: 33 1 42 78 00 30
MÉTRO: Temple

A walk through the *Marais,* from the southern portion surrounding *Saint-Gervais* to the north—*Synagogue de Nazareth* near *Place de la République*—is rich in pleasures as well as contradictions. The narrow, picturesque streets running past elegant and ancient buildings, with beautifully carved doorways; unusual shops, a diverse beauty of art and commerce and people: I was stunned throughout my first walk here, years ago. Kept stopping to stare.

There is also ruin, hidden away. The first time I roamed streets in the northern section of the *Marais,* heading away from *Saint-Gervais,* exploring at random, no map in hand, noting such street names as *rue Charlot, rue Saintonge, rue des Rosiers* (a culinary paradise of Jewish food), *rue Pavée, rue de Poitou, rue des Haudriettes, rue de Parc Royal, rue Pastourelle* (laid out in the thirteenth century)—I passed as much dilapidation as high maintenance.

But following so many streetscapes, years ago and now, zigzagging between south and north, I felt an insistent liveliness of being. The *Marais* is ancient ground. In the beginning it was home to religious foundations. Now, on weekdays, sometimes there are no people in sight; on weekend nights the streets are crowded with tourists, revelers in gay bars, parents pushing strollers. The display windows of art galleries, contemporary fashion, artisans' workshops, eclectic bookshops, antique shops, luxury boutiques (585 euros for designer sneakers), kosher restaurants. Museums. Cafés on *rue de Bretagne,* falafel stalls on *rue des Rosiers,* the main street of the old Jewish quarter and still a center of Jewish culture and delicious food. There's a glut of clothing shops. Except for the pockets of gentrification—which native Parisians do not care for—these streets have an identity at once scarred and glorious with centuries of history, use, of human habitation, aristocratic classicism, working-class energy, failure, murder. Renewal and renovation were the obsession of André Malraux, de Gaulle's minister of cultural affairs in the sixties; old-time Parisians (according to Eric Hazan's brilliant *The Invention of Paris: A History in Footsteps*) do not approve of how Malraux sanitized this ancient *quartier*. "*The Marais has lost its soul,*" one resident declared.

The *Marais*—or *marshland or swamp*—became habitable around the twelfth century when the Knights Templar and other religious communities arrived here and drained the swampy ground where sheep grazed, market gardens thrived, and arable land became available. There's also evidence of earlier habitation in the sixth century.

Kings and nobles built elegant *hôtels* throughout the sixteenth century, and *King Henri IV, le vert Galant,* designed the *Place Royale* (1605) in gorgeous white and red stone—later called *Place des Vosges*—before he was assassinated in 1610. Literary salons were the platforms of Molière (see p. 144), Madame de Sévigné (*Letters*), Madame de La Fayette (*La Princesse de Clèves,* 1678), and Cardinal Richelieu, who gathered with the *salonnards* in the nighttime town houses where they read their latest manuscripts aloud and made the smart set laugh and blush. The *Place des Vosges* was the fun part of town.

Beautiful museums would eventually take over some of the largest *hôtels*: the sixteenth-century *Hôtel Carnavalet* (where Madame de Sévigné lived) became the museum of the city of Paris; *Thorigny,* the *Picasso* museum; the *Hôtel de Saint-Aignan* became the superb *Musée d'Art et d'Histoire du Judaïsme* on the west side of **rue du Temple**; the *Hôtel de Sully* on **rue Saint-Antoine** (with an **Orangerie** and a first-rate bookshop off its front garden, *Librairie des Monuments Nationaux*; open Tues–Sun), leads through an archway in the northeast corner of the garden, another entrance to *Place des Vosges.*

By the next century, the *Marais* was dying. Then it was abandoned by artists and the rich for *Saint-Germain.* Many of the *hôtels particulaires* went to seed, slowly turning into slum dwellings for immigrants fleeing the poverty and pogroms in the East. Schools, tenements, stables, broken-down workshops took over many streets, newcomers throughout the nineteenth century crowding into dark and moldering buildings. Artisans—furniture makers, leather and jewelry craftsmen, metalworkers, clothiers—found cheap rents for their large families as well as "studios" for their work, ramshackle workspaces along *rue Saint-Antoine* in the eleventh *arrondissement.* Novelist Nancy Huston sets *The Mark of the Angel* in these backstreets. Jews from the East made a living and also created a community where their friends and relatives from home had already preceded them. They went to synagogue. Institutional Judaism was well represented in the *Marais,* on *rue Pavée,* for instance—and a pretty tall Art Nouveau synagogue by Hector Guimard is open to visitors on Friday nights for services at 8 along *rue des Tournelles.*

Ten minutes to the north, there's the oldest of the great synagogues in Paris, *Synagogue Nazareth* (1852).

DIRECTIONS: *Synagogue Nazareth* stands toward the top of the south side of *rue Notre-Dame de Nazareth* (no. 15), about a block to the west off the lovely *Temple Square* (not far from *Place de la République*). If you've been walking north from *SOMA* (the neighborhood of *Saint-Gervais*), keep walking north along the west side of *Temple Square*; cross *rue du Temple* from its west side as you pass the church of Saint-Elizabeth. *Synagogue Nazareth* is about half a block down rue *Notre-Dame de Nazareth,* on your left as you walk west.

I arrived too late for Shabbat on a Saturday morning, but the rabbis admitted me as *kiddush* was in progress. *Kiddush* is the Hebrew word for "sanctification," a blessing recited over wine or grape juice to sanctify the **Shabbat** and Jewish holidays. Additionally, the word refers to a small repast held on **Shabbat** or festival mornings after the prayer services. *Kaffeeklatsch* will also do.

I crossed the spacious lobby, just inside the synagogue's front doors, and was permitted to go through the swinging doors into the synagogue itself. Just as I saw at the Friday night evening service in the *Grande Synagogue* (see p. 169), the worship space was beautiful, but *Nazareth* is not as large as *la Victoire*. The circles of blue stained glass on the ceiling, like rose windows, embedded with Stars of David; the double (two-story) galleries, with cast-iron columns, painted in blue and mellow yellow, screened with handmade lace; the multiple chandeliers of light; the ark at the unifying head, like a watchful eye. The ceiling was not as high as the *Grande Synagogue*'s, the aisles were narrower.

Tikkun olam: the Hebrew words meaning the "repair of the world" came into my head, a memory of the social justice movements in New York City where the Jewish community and individual Jews have often taken the lead. These words expressed the purpose of this holy place.

Returning to the large lobby, I found the *kiddush* proceeding with warmth and high spirits. No churchy whispering here. The men sipping the wine, eating from the buffet, you could tell they were friends. I remembered the emphasis on relationship and reciprocity expressed by the Jewish prophet Martin Buber, whose classic *I and Thou* had been assigned in college philosophy and theology classes. Buber's dialogic theology/psychology—

> *The basic word I-You can be spoken only with one's whole being . . .*
> > *I require a You to become; becoming I, I say You.*
> > *All actual life is encounter.*

The world is holy because it is where we encounter God, as Adam Kirsch puts it in his review of a new biography of Buber by Paul Mendes-Flohr, *Martin Buber: A Life of Faith and Dissent*. The God Buber describes is

> *neither a stern lawgiver nor a merciful redeemer but a close presence to whom we can always turn for intimacy . . .*

Buber (1878–1965) woke us up as undergraduates, inspired activism, reaching out to communities in need of help.

Best known for his revival of Hasidism, a mystical movement out of eastern Europe in the eighteenth and nineteenth centuries, that vision was one of the sources of Buber's "I-Thou" philosophy.

A few times that Saturday morning, people asked me where I was from.

New York? The greatest!

Again, as at *la Victoire,* they approved. They were open and friendly, bringing back to me the Seders I'd gone to on Passover in New York, the hosts' radical hospitality to the stranger, the good food, the good cheer. The warmth of the relationships among the guests.

Nearby

TEMPLE SQUARE, OR SQUARE DU TEMPLE: *A pretty, quiet garden with a pool of flowing water; a rock garden; benches where readers of Sunday morning newspapers predominate along with small children on monkey bars; great clusters of singing birds; spirea, lilacs, and flowering cherry trees in spring. In 1140 this was the headquarters of the Knights Templar and in 1792 the site of the Temple keep where the king and queen were held before their execution not far away in Place de la Concorde. Cafés on the south side on **rue de Bretagne.***

CAFÉ CHARLOT: *38, rue de Bretagne. Classic brasserie. Good food, service. Crowded on weekends.*

EMMAÜS ALTERNATIVE: *74, rue de Turbigo. On the street behind **rue de Notre-Dame de Nazareth**, near the corner. The large black-and-white photo of Abbé Pierre (see p. 52) in the* *window locates you in one of his Goodwill-type thrift shops. Good variety: much clothing and accessories, men and women's, children's, toys, furniture, household, books.*

SPF: *Secours Populaire Français (French Popular Relief)*—**9, 11, rue Froissart.** *Open Mon—Fri, 8—7:30. Secourspopulaire.fr. Tel: 33 1 44 78 21 00. Walk east for five minutes on rue de Bretagne, the south side of Temple Square. No. 9, 11, **rue Frois-**sart is on your right.* **Motto: All that is human is ours.** *National Association in the spirit of the Universal Declaration of Human Rights. Founded August 1, 1944. French nonprofit, international charitable relief in opposition to discrimination, poverty, child abuse, hunger, homelessness. Many volunteers from local* quartiers, *especially in winter. Ask for the excellent guidebook; it lists all the social services available through* **SPF,** *with telephone numbers, websites, addresses, and hours of operation. Ring the bell and wait for admission.*

Related Reading

Gershom Scholem, *Major Trends in Jewish Mysticism*

Robert Alter, *Necessary Angels: Tradition and Modernity in Kafka, Benjamin, and Scholem*

Martin Buber, *I and Thou*

Paul Mendes-Flohr, *Martin Buber: A Life of Faith and Dissent*

Saint-Germain de Charonne

SAINT-GERMAIN DE CHARONNE

LOCATION: 111, RUE DE BAGNOLET (ON PLACE SAINT-
BLAISE)
HOURS: Mon–Sat, 8:30–7; Sun, 9–1
MÉTRO: Porte de Bagnolet; Alexandre Dumas; Gambetta
WWW.SAINTGERMAINDECHARONNE.FR

The church is simple, a small Romanesque gem, in *quartier* Saint-Blaise, with a twelfth-century bell tower. It
stands at the crest of the village high street—*Place Saint-
Blaise*—in the ancient village of *Charonne*. *(Walk up rue de
Bagnolet—northeast—from the Alexandre Dumas métro.)*

I have never seen another soul inside this church (recently
opened after a years-long restoration) nor have I attended a
service here, though I'd like to. It's beautifully cool in summer, like all the small stone churches in France. The church
feels full of grace; you can feel the stillness, the language of
prayer. On the rear wall of this ancient chapel, directly opposite the altar, is a painting of *Saint Germain* meeting the child
Saint Geneviève on the road from Nanterre and blessing her.
He tells her to go to Paris and enter a convent, or so the legend goes. There's been a church here since the ninth century.

The modern drama of *Saint-Germain de Charonne*
is commemorated in the *Charonne Cemetery* behind the
church.

DIRECTIONS: To enter through the rear entrance, from the
Gambetta Place métro, walk down *rue Stendhal* and descend

the staircase alongside pretty houses until you reach the gate. Or to enter from the front, ascend the old stone staircase to the left of the church entrance—passing the flowering cherry trees in April—and you're there.

On your right (or left, depending on whether you entered from the front or the rear), in the front row of the middle of the graveyard, is the headstone that is part of the history of World War II in Paris, specifically the Nazi Occupation, and the *"Purges"*— *l'épuration sauvage*—that followed Germany's defeat and withdrawal from Paris in August 1944. The headstone is inscribed with the name *Robert Brasillach,* who was convicted of treason in January 1945 and sentenced to death. Fifty-nine prominent writers, including Valéry, Claudel, Colette, Paulhan, led by *résistant* and prolific Catholic novelist François Mauriac, signed a petition for mercy. Mercy for *Brasillach.*

The petition provoked an intense public debate in the newspapers between Mauriac and Albert Camus. Justice must prevail over charity, was Camus's view. *Brasillach* was scum; he had betrayed some of Camus's closest *résistant* friends, men with families, who were shot summarily. *"Every time I talk about justice, M. Mauriac talks of charity,"* wrote Camus.

But in the end, hating the very principle of the death penalty, that the State had the authority to take a life, as well as how vicious the vengeful *Purges* had become, Camus changed his mind. As historian Julian Jackson puts it, *"he judged Mauriac to have been right."* Deciding for mercy— (mercy, Camus decided, with Mauriac, was the most profound virtue, the opposite of the force that was now destroying the spiritual fabric of Europe and clearly the heart of the religion practiced in France)—Camus signed Mauriac's petition.

Paris was torn apart by the case. Those who sought a pardon for *Brasillach,* a fanatic fascist, argued that other writers/collaborators had done far worse during the war than this silly *normalien.* (He was widely assumed to be homosexual.)

Some background.

After the Liberation in August 1944, the wild nights and days of rejoicing, the triumphal return of Charles de Gaulle marching down the Champs Élysées to the *Cathedral of Notre-Dame* and the welcome of one million Parisians, there came a shift. A powerful mood of vengeance against the Parisians who had collaborated with the Nazis ruled the streets of Paris. The women who'd slept with them, guilty of "horizontal collaboration," had their heads shaved, swastikas tattooed on their cheeks, bodies stripped naked and paraded through the city. The writers and journalists who had expressed praise of the German enemy, publishing in Nazi periodicals and being paid by Nazi editors, were arrested. Many were tried for treason in French courts, and judged, based on Article 75 of the French penal code, which condemned treason and sharing information with the enemy. Many were pardoned by de Gaulle or received light jail sentences. Some were executed.

The story of *Brasillach* is more of a moral drama than a political showdown.

He grew up as one of the young literary prodigies for which Paris is famous. Brilliant at fifteen, widely read, contemptuous of the left, absolutely certain of his right-wing take on politics, culture, literature—a loudmouthed and public anti-Semite, he wrote bad fascist novels—a passionate intellectual in the mold of the elite students at the École normale supérieure. *Les normaliens* (Jean-Paul Sartre, Georges Pompidou, Maurice Merleau-Ponty, Simone de Beauvoir, Simone Weil) were his peers, the adolescent intellectual elite (like their equivalents at Harvard, Oxford, and Cambridge). He had his heart set on "a fascist future for France," to quote Alice Kaplan, whose book *The Collaborator: The Trial and Execution of Robert Brasillach* is an excellent overview of **Brasillach**'s prewar world and its aftermath in Liberation Paris.

Brasillach was a sort of enfant terrible in the thirties, considered brilliant by his fellow fascists and anti-Semites on the Left Bank; leftists and liberals considered him ridiculous. He was short and chubby, spectacled, clever. A prankster. His allegiance with the Nazis after the Occupation surprised no one. He loved the Germans, their law-and-order mystique; their hatred for the mess of French democracy and for an evolving, always reforming Christianity, which **Brasillach** loathed. A law-and-order fascist religion suited him fine.

His collaboration after 1940 took vicious forms: he denounced whoever he knew was *résistant* or a critic of the Germans, who in turn entertained him, published him, made him editor of *Je suis partout*, an extremely fascist journal. He urged the Nazis to not only murder the Jews but not to spare their children. He horrified the French; but some applauded his extremism.

So when the war was over, he was dragged out of his hiding place in a maid's room on **rue du Tournon** and tried for treason. A large number of the attendees at his trial cheered for him.

But the jury and the judges were not moved by the defendant's cult of cleverness or the number of his publications, the amusing boy (he was thirty-five) who hated Jews and would say anything, the more hate-filled the better. The patriotism of Hate Speech.

Mauriac brought his petition for "Mercy for Brasillach" in person to de Gaulle. (Readers of Mauriac's masterpiece, *The Knot of Vipers*, know how he saw vengeance as the sign of Satan corrupting the soul.) Mauriac and then Camus saw the vengeance of the *Purges* as the final corruption of the soul of France, a revisiting of the Dreyfus Affair (see p. 172).

Mauriac was the writer de Gaulle said he most admired. But he refused his petition. Though a faithful Catholic himself, he refused to show mercy. *Brasillach* was executed on February 6, 1945, and buried here in *Charonne* in this peaceful pastoral setting.

Simone de Beauvoir disapproved of the death sentence and the execution of the boy wonder: It turned a villain into a martyr.

As you sit in the *cemetery of Charonne,* on the outskirts of a working-class neighborhood, the place silent and empty though lovely with roses in spring and summer, you might realize that the name *Brasillach* did not die on the day he was executed and buried here. His politics did not die (Holocaust denial, anti-immigration, extreme nationalism). But France abolished the death penalty in 1981, with Robert Badinter, Minister of Justice, as advocate for the legislation of mercy.

Nearby

LE MERLE MOQUEUR: *Walk down the hill from the church to 51, rue du Bagnolet. A large bookstore (*librairie*) with a strong children's section. Readings, discussion groups, information from the staff. www.lemerlemoquer.fr. The shop and the old cobblestone streets surrounding it have a friendly small-town intimacy.*

MSF (MÉDECINS SANS FRONTIÈRES): *8, rue Saint-Sabin. Tel: 00 33 1 48 06 68 68. Founded in Paris in 1971, by Bernard*

Kouchner, **MSF** *is an international medical humanitarian organization that helps wherever need is greatest—epidemics, injustice—with emergency medical aid and basic health care. Offices in twenty-one countries. In 1999* **MSF** *was awarded the Nobel Peace Prize.* **Walk southwest**—*walking takes less time than the métro—from* **Saint-Germain de Charonne** *as far as the Bastille area (about twenty-five minutes). Bear right at boulevard Richard Lenoir; a block north you'll find* **8, rue Saint-Sabin:** *you're in Old Paris—colorful, crowded, and gritty. At* **MSF** *you can talk to staff and sit in on staff meetings. Call ahead for schedules of meetings or visit to find out. We spent two hours observing a spirited training session for volunteers about to leave for Africa. Volunteers ages eighteen to fifty.*

In the offices of **MSF**, *you are visiting* **Sacred Paris:** *where humanists or ordinary volunteers locate a sacred presence in humanity itself; in actions of generosity, courage, and decency; in the human urge to help, despite risks and doubt and fear. Watch the excellent video: "Once Upon a Time, the MSF."*

SAINT-AMBROISE: ***www.saint-ambroise.com. 71 bis, boulevard Voltaire.*** *Walk north (fifteen minutes) from* **rue Saint-Sabin,** *along* **boulevard Richard Lenoir.** *You'll run right into* **boulevard Voltaire** *at the intersection. When you see how the church rises over the boulevard and the newly planted park across from it, you may think of how the church of* **la Trinité** *in the ninth arrondissement has a similar effect. No mystery:* **Théodore Ballu** *was also the architect of* **Saint-Ambroise** *(1863–1869). Both his churches manifest dignity and beauty from their* petit monceau. *Named after the saint of Milan, Ambrose, who baptized Saint Augustine, this church, according to its parish booklet, has enough outreach into the parish and the surrounding neighborhood of the eleventh* arrondissement *to support a small city. The one regular event that brings in the crowds is the Sunday afternoon concerts (twice a month, between 3 and 5). In 2019, just before the pandemic, I heard a beautiful performance of Bach's Cantata for the Feast of the Ascension.*

*The **Saint-Ambroise** ministry has mounted powerful exhibits regarding the Civil War in Algeria in the nineties when terrorists kidnapped (and later beheaded) seven French Trappist monks of the Tibhirine monastery in the Atlas Mountains. The story of the friendship between the Christian monks and the Muslim villagers is extremely moving. (The commercial movie,* Of Gods and Men, *won the Grand Prix at Cannes in 2010.) In 2018 the monks were beatified in Rome.*

OXFAM: *8, rue Saint-Ambroise. Walk up the hill to the left of the church, facing it from **boulevard Voltaire**. **Oxfam la Bouquinerie** (old bookstore) sells—besides books—CDs, DVDs, clothes, toys, housewares. Pleasant ambiance. All items are secondhand, given by artisans who have restored them. Artisans du Monde (world's craftsmen), pioneers of fair trade, was created by Abbé Pierre (see p. 52), opening its doors in 1974, dedicated to the support of solidarity and human rights. www .oxfamfrance.org/magasins/bouquinerie-oxfam-paris-saint -ambroise/; Oxfam.glparis@gmail.com.*

OXYMORE: *60 rue Saint-Maur. Walk one block further up from Oxfam on **rue Saint-Ambroise** and you'll come upon this first-rate **Italian** bistro) on the east side of the street. Sometimes crowded. Sidewalk seating. A friendly neighborhood spot.*

MEZZE DU LIBAN: *48 bis, **rue Saint-Maur**. Delicious Lebanese food. Friendly service. Crowded at lunchtime and some evenings.*

SQUARE MAURICE-GARDETTE: *So lovely, at all times of day. Two thousand plantings of great variety. An abundance of chestnuts, magnolias, sycamore, palms; a massive canopy of trees above the flower beds of lilies, roses, irises. Children having fun,* as the Austrian journalist Joseph Roth wrote in "The Child in Paris": "the consequence of the warm, loving, nurturing softness in the way they are brought up."

A bronze sculpture by Jacques Perrin: **Le Botteleur.** *Many* résistants—*including Maurice Gardette (1895–1941), who lived nearby in the eleventh* arrondissement *and was shot by the Nazis, with twenty-six of his comrades. More Jews were deported from the eleventh than from any other* arrondissement. **En-trances on rue Lacharrière; rue Rochebrune; rue du Général Guilhem; rue du Général Blaise. Métro: rue Saint-Maur; Saint-Ambroise.**

Related Reading

Barbara Will, *Unlikely Collaboration: Gertrude Stein, Bernard Faÿ, and the Vichy Dilemma*

Robert Zaretsky, *A Life Worth Living: Albert Camus and the Quest for Meaning*

Susan Zuccotti, *The Holocaust, the French, and the Jews*

John W. Kiser, *The Monks of Tibhirine: Faith, Love, and Terror in Algeria*

ACKNOWLEDGMENTS

Many friends and colleagues have shared their knowledge of hidden places in the City of Light: *Suzanne Ranoux*, throughout the research and writing of my first two Paris books—and now *Sacred Paris*—has been so knowledgeable and warmhearted, the perfect Parisian friend to share long lunches and dinners with, all the while talking about and describing the city that might as well be a member of her own family. *Mathieu Ranoux*, also a lifelong Parisian, has been a discerning resource of French history and culture.

Jo Lowery, of American University in Paris, has been a delightful companion and connoisseur of the *Onzieme*. *Veronica Pollard*, of New York and Paris, guided me through *quartiers* I would not have found on my own: *The Parc Martin Luther King* in *les Batignolles*, a delightful green space in the seventeenth *arrondissement* with a delightful restaurant, aptly named *Coretta*.

Jack Becker and his wife, *Clare Hahn*, cherished and retold their memories of Paris in their youth. *Miriam Luisi* and *Robert Pollock*, with whom we dined in the middle of the night at the old *Les Halles*, had this city written on their hearts. This is true, too, of *Bill and Judith Moyers; Warren and Stephanie Cohen;* the late *Elizabeth Cullinan; Donald Spoto*, the inspiring author of the biography *Joan: The Mysterious Life of the Heretic Who Became a Saint; Paul Dinter;*

Betsy Blachly and Henry Chapin; Armand Jayet; the late *Allon Schoener* of New York City and Los Angeles; novelists *Frances Hill and Leon Arden* of London and Connecticut; *Nancy Lefenfeld,* author of *The Fate of Others,* a history of the Jewish Resistance in France in the Second World War; *Gary Ostrower,* legendary history professor at Alfred University and his wife, Judge *Judith Samber; Anne Barlborough* of Quin, Ireland, and *Michelle Marlborough* of Galway. My conversations with *Professor Emeritus David Kleinbard* of the City University of New York, writer and friend, have given me the gifts of his knowledge of *Zadoc Kahn* in Paris; like his memories of the late *Maureen Waters,* they are embedded in his heart. Editor *Susanna Porter* put into my hands the superb book by *Alexander Lobrano, Hungry for Paris.* The poetry of *Catherine de Vinck,* a transcendent and lifelong celebration of the Light, was born in Paris as the Second World War was winding down. *Sally Cunneen* and *Joe Cunneen,* founding publishers of *Cross Currents,* introduced me to that protector of immigrants, the ancient church of *Saint-Merri* on the Right Bank. *Anne Herlick, Burt Visotsky,* and *Carole Zylberstein-Hillman* have enriched my encounters with the synagogues of Paris. *Karen Hillman* helped me connect with the very generous Carole Hillman.

Last but not least, there is the late Lois Wallace, my first agent, another lover of the City of Light.

The New York Society Library in New York City, under the guidance of *Carolyn Waters,* has made my work move along with a delightful efficiency. As have the city's independent bookstores: *Book Culture* on the Upper West Side; the *Strand; Shakespeare & Company.* In Paris, the presence of such bookshops as the *Abbey* with Brian Spence; *Shake-*

speare & Company with Linda; Galignani with the buyer, Anna. WHSmith; and Imagigraphe in rue Oberkampf.

At **St. Martin's Press,** I have once again enjoyed the enthusiasm and support of my editor, *Charles Spicer.* He and his assistant, *Sarah Grill,* worked so smoothly within the constraints of a pandemic and a home office. It makes a huge difference to me that Charlie knows and loves Paris. I write, too, in memory of the late *Matthew Shear,* publisher at St. Martin's, who cheered me on with my first Paris book, *The Hidden Gardens of Paris. Robert Grom* is the wonderful art director who has made each of the covers of the Paris books a truly splendid creation. Many thanks also to *Elizabeth Catalano, Adriana Coada,* interior designers *Fritz Metsch,* and *Nicola Ferguson, Ginny Perrin, David Burr, Sara Beth Haring,* and *Sarah Schoof* for your immeasurable help and support.

John Thornton, my agent, has always been an insightful participant in the world of publishing books: I am so grateful for his help.

My son, *Joseph Cahill,* and *ma belle fille, Marion Ranoux,* once again the extraordinarily talented photographer of this book as well as of *The Hidden Gardens of Paris* and *The Streets of Paris,* have given me the hospitality of the most generous order; they have also guided me all over the city, the off-the-beaten-track city that only local residents know and appreciate. Of the greatest importance, Joseph has acted as my computer mentor, an impossible task given my estrangement from the world of technology. So many thanks for your patience, grace, and competence; **without you this book would not have come to life.** *Sacred Paris* is the product of your technological expertise and *Marion's* photography, and daughter Nina's joie de vivre. I am so grateful to each of you.

In New York City, my daughter, Kristin Cahill, has

made many practical transactions easier for me than they might have been. Her family—James, Devlin, Lucia, and Conor—is, like Paris, another collective love of my life.

At home in New York has been all along my husband, Tom, with whom I first saw Paris. Not only his memories but his affection for the city enrich mine, especially because our beloved son, Joseph, now lives there with his wife and our beautiful granddaughter.

With gratitude and love I offer all of you *Sacred Paris*, this book that survived the challenges and difficulties of work in spite of the pandemic.

SOURCES

Azimi, Roxana, and Stéphanie Le Bars. "La cathédrale Notre-Dame de Paris, une passion américaine," *Le Magazine du Monde,* May 31, 2019.

Berger, John. *About Looking,* 1991.

Bokenkotter, Thomas. *Church and Revolution: Catholics in the Struggle for Democracy and Social Justice,* 1998.

Bonhoeffer, Dietrich. *Letters and Papers from Prison,* 1953.

Boudet, Philippe, and Guy Latge. *Guide du Paris Monastique de Lutèce à la Révolution,* 2009.

Brown, Frederick. *For the Soul of France: Culture Wars in the Age of Dreyfus,* 2010.

———. *Zola: A Life,* 1995.

Buber, Martin. *I and Thou,* trans. Walter Kaufmann, 1970.

Cahill, Susan. *Hidden Gardens of Paris: A Guide to the Parks, Squares, and Woodlands of the City of Light,* 2012.

———. *The Streets of Paris: A Guide to the City of Light Following in the Footsteps of Famous Parisians Throughout History,* 2017.

———, ed. *Wise Women: Over Two Thousand Years of Spiritual Writing by Women.* 1996.

———, ed. *Women & Fiction: Short Stories By and About Women,* vols. 1–6, 1975–2002.

Carrère, Emmanuel. *The Kingdom,* trans. John Lambert, 2014.

Casevecchie, Janine. *Paris médiéval,* 2009.

Castor, Helen. *Joan of Arc: A History,* 2014.

Chazan, Robert. "Trial, Condemnation, and Censorship: The Talmud in Medieval Europe." In *The Trial of the Talmud: Paris, 1240,* 2012.

Cobb, Richard. *Paris and Elsewhere: Selected Writings,* 1998.

Cole, Henri. *Orphic Paris,* 2018.

DeJean, Joan. *How Paris Became Paris: The Invention of the Modern City*, 2014.

Delacroix, Eugène. *The Journal of Eugène Delacroix: A Selection*, ed. Hubert Wellington, trans. Lucy Norton, 2004.

Desmard, Laurent. *Abbé Pierre: Images d'une vie*, 2006.

Desmons, Gilles. *Walking Paris: Thirty Original Walks in and Around Paris*, 1999.

Duchen, Jessica. *Gabriel Fauré*, 2000.

Dumas, Alexandre. *La Reine Margot*, 1845; reprint, revised trans. David Coward, 2008.

Duras, Marguerite. *Practicalities: Marguerite Duras Speaks to Jérôme Beaujour*, trans. Barbara Bray, 1987.

Druon, Maurice. *The History of Paris from Caesar to Saint Louis*, 1966.

Eagleton, Terry. *Reason, Faith, and Revolution: Reflections on the God Debate*, 2009.

Eco, Umberto, ed. "Cathedral of Notre Dame." In *History of Beauty*, 2002.

Eisler, Benita. *Chopin's Funeral*, 2003.

Ellsberg, Robert. *All Saints: Daily Reflections on Saints, Prophets, and Witnesses for Our Time*, 1997.

Ferry, Luc. *A Brief History of Thought: A Philosophical Guide to Living*, 2011.

Flaubert, Gustave. "The Legend of Saint Julien the Hospitaller," in *Three Tales*, 1877; reprint trans. A. J. Krailsheimer, 1999.

Fournier, Jacques. *Saint-Roch*, 2011.

Gay, Peter. *Mozart: A Life*, 1999.

Giorgi, Rosa. *Angels and Demons in Art*, 2005.

Gogh, Vincent van. *The Letters: The Complete Illustrated and Annotated Edition*, ed. Leo Jansen, Jans Luijten, and Nienke Bakker, 2009.

Goldstone, Nancy. *The Rival Queens: Catherine de' Medici, Her Daughter Marguerite de Valois, and the Betrayal That Ignited a Kingdom*, 2015.

Gray-Durant, Delia. *Blue Guide to Paris*, 2015.

Green, Julian. *Paris*, 2012.

Harris, Ruth. *Dreyfus: Politics, Emotion, and the Scandal of the Century*, 2010.

Hazan, Eric. *The Invention of Paris: A History in Footsteps*, 2010.

Hirshfield, Jane, ed. *Women in Praise of the Sacred: 43 Centuries of Spiritual Poetry by Women*, 1994.

Holloway, Richard. *A Little History of Religion*, 2016.

Horne, Alistair. *Seven Ages of Paris*, 2002.

———. *La Belle France: A Short History*, 2005.

Hugo, Victor. *The Hunchback of Notre-Dame*, 1831; trans. Catherine Liu, 2002.

Jackson, Julian. *De Gaulle*, 2018.

———. *France: The Dark Years, 1940–1944*, 2001.

James, Henry. *The Ambassadors*, 1903.

James, William. *The Varieties of Religious Experience*, 1902; reprint 1961.

Johnson, Paul. *Mozart*, 2013.

Jones, Colin. *Paris: The Biography of a City*, 2004.

Kaag, John. *Sick Souls, Healthy Minds: How William James Can Save Your Life*, 2020.

Kahn, Robert, ed. *City Secrets Paris: The Essential Insider's Guide*, 2014.

Kaplan, Alice. *The Collaborator: The Trial and Execution of Robert Brasillach*, 2000.

Kauffmann, Jean-Paul. *The Struggle with the Angel: Delacroix, Jacob, and the God of Good and Evil*, 2001; reprint trans. Patricia Clancy, 2002.

Kearney, Richard, ed. *Reimagining the Sacred: Richard Kearney Debates God*, 2016.

Kirsch, Adam. "Modernity, Faith, and Martin Buber," *New Yorker*, May 6, 2019.

Knez, Julien. *Paris: Fenêtres sur l'Histoire. De la Commune à mai 68*, 2016.

Küng, Hans. *The Catholic Church, A Short History*, trans. John Bowden, 2001.

Lacouture, Jean. *Jesuits: A Multibiography*, 1991; reprint trans. Jeremy Leggatt, 1995.

Landes, Alison, and Sonia Landes. *Pariswalks: Close-ups of the Left Bank*, 1975.

Lubac, Henri de. *The Faith of Teilhard de Chardin*. trans. René Hague, 1965.

MacCulloch, Diarmaid. *Christianity: The First Three Thousand Years*, 2009.

Marissen, Michael. *Bach & God*, 2016.

Martines, Lauro. *Furies: War in Europe: 1450–1700*, 2013.

Marty, Martin. *The Christian World: A Global History*, 2007.

Mendes-Flohr, Paul. *Martin Buber: A Life of Faith and Dissent*, 2019.

McNamara, Denis R. *How to Read Churches: A Guide to Ecclesiastical Architecture*, 2011.

Molière: 5 Plays, trans. Richard Wilbur and Alan Drury, 1982.

———. *The Misanthrope and Other Plays*, trans. Donald M. Frame, 1968.

Naifeh, Steven, and Gregory White Smith. *Van Gogh: The Life*, 2012.

Nairn, Ian. *Nairn's Paris*, 1968.

Nectoux, Jean-Michel, ed. *Gabriel Fauré: His Life Through His Letters*, 1980; reprint trans. J. A. Underwood, 1984.

Pétrement, Simone. *Simone Weil: A Life*, 1976.

Read, Piers Paul. *The Dreyfus Affair: The Scandal That Tore France in Two*, 2012.

Roe, Sue. *The Private Lives of the Impressionists*, 2006.

Rowe, Nina. *The Jew, the Cathedral and the Medieval City: Synagoga and Ecclesia in the Thirteenth Century*, 2011.

Ruelle, Karen Gray, and Deborah Durland DeSaix. *The Grand Mosque of Paris: A Story of How Muslims Rescued Jews During the Holocaust*, 2008.

Schama, Simon. *Landscape and Memory*, 1994.

Sciolino, Elaine. *The Seine: The River That Made Paris*, 2020.

Seward, Desmond. *The First Bourbon: Henri IV, King of France and Navarre*, 1971.

Silverman, Debora. *Van Gogh and Gauguin: The Search for Sacred Art*, 2000.

Smart, Ninian. *The Religious Experience*, 1991.

Smith, Rollin. *Louis Vierne: Organist of Notre Dame Cathedral*, 1999.

Spoto, Donald. *Joan: The Mysterious Life of the Heretic Who Became a Saint*, 2007.

Taylor, Charles. "What Does Secularism Mean?" in *Dilemmas and Connections: Selected Essays*, 2011.

Teilhard de Chardin, Pierre. *Letters to Two Friends 1926–1952*, trans. Helen Weaver, 1957.

——. *The Divine Milieu: An Essay on the Interior Life*, 1957.

Temko, Allan. *Notre-Dame of Paris*, 1955.

Trouilleux, Rodolphe. *Unexplored Paris*, trans. Patricia Abbou and David Cox, 2019.

Villon, François. *Poems of François Villon*, trans. Peter Dale, 2001.

Weil, Simone. *Waiting for God*, trans. Emma Crawford, 1951.

——. *Gravity and Grace*, trans. Arthur Wills, 1952; reprint 1997.

Wills, Garry. "My Koran Problem," *New York Review of Books*, March 24, 2016.

INDEX

ABOUT THE AUTHOR

Susan Cahill has published other travel books about Paris: the acclaimed *Hidden Gardens of Paris*—"No matter how many times you have been to Paris," said Bill Moyers, "never go without Susan Cahill"—and *The Streets of Paris*—"this elegantly written book is absolutely essential reading for all travelers bound for Paris," said Alexander Lobrano. Italy, the focus of *Desiring Italy*, features women writers celebrating a Country and a Culture. *The Smiles of Rome*—"original," "irresistible," "fascinating," said the *New York Times*.

With her husband, the writer Tom Cahill, author of *How the Irish Saved Civilization*, she lived in Ireland, producing with him the acclaimed *A Literary Guide to Ireland*. Later she compiled *For the Love of Ireland*, "a delightful book." She is the author of the novel *Earth Angels*, editor of the six-volume Women and Fiction series and of the anthology *Wise Women: Over Two Thousand Years of Spiritual Writing by Women*. "Every collection of Susan Cahill has been outstanding in its quality and originality. I feel it an honor to appear in this one," wrote the late Tillie Olsen.

Cahill lives in New York City with her husband, Tom, and visits Paris in every season.

ABOUT THE PHOTOGRAPHER

Marion Ranoux is a freelance photographer (*Hidden Gardens of Paris: A Guide to the Parks, Squares, and Woodlands of the City of Light; The Streets of Paris: Following in the Footsteps of Famous Parisians Throughout History*); staff member at AUP, the American University in Paris; and translator of Czech literature, including Ludvík Vaculík. A lifelong Parisian, she has done graduate work in visual history at the École des Hautes Études en Sciences Sociales (EHESS). She loves to walk her city and take photographs.